I0035423

The Hidden Figures

The Women who Crunched the Numbers in Civility, Entrepreneurship, Philanthropy, Nonprofit, and Authorship

Dr Nadia Anthony

Copyright © 2021 Dr Nadia Anthony

All rights reserved. No part of this publication may be reproduced, distributed, or transmitted in any form or by any means, including photocopying, recording, or any other electronic or mechanical methods, without the prior written permission of the publisher, except in the case of brief quotations embodied in critical reviews and certain other noncommercial uses permitted by copyright law. For permission, write to the publisher at:

Greatness University Publishers
London, UK
www.greatnessuniversity.co.uk

ISBN: 978-1-913164-35-5
ISBN-13: 978-1-913164-35-5

DEDICATION

I would like to dedicate this book to my grandmother "The Hidden Figure" that has been discovered by her Granddaughter. Message to my sweet grandmother: You have retired from your career but you have not retired from the lives of woman. You have been a "Hidden Figure" for years. If no one has seen your work, the lord grants you as astronaut of the year.

I love you!

I dedicate this book to you Blanche Crockett.

CONTENTS

ACKNOWLEDGMENTS

I would like to express my special thanks of gratitude to every woman that allowed themselves to be lifted in this book. The Hidden Figures Book has become a golden opportunity to do future projects, women retreats and other anthologies. Thank you for unveiling your hard work and testimonies.

Foreword

Professor Ona C. Miller

Foreword

Hidden Figures are those that are rarely noticed or acknowledged. They are also the ones that probably would rather stay in the background rather than out front. They are the leaders that are crucial to the existence of everything that happens in the world, but yet are not necessarily visible, or at least they may think that they are not. But, the reality is that most Hidden Figures are the essential elements of the equations. Although society, culture, and traditions have trained us to accept their categorical perspectives that leave us in the background, the truth is we are not the background. We are the foundation by which all things are built.

We are women Hidden Figures created to bring forth, produce life, and initiate creation upon the earth and in the world. We nurture, cultivate, curate, and incubate the very needs that are present today. We have learned that it is not necessary to lead from the front, but we understand that the best leader can lead from any position. Nevertheless, many of us as women often wonder if what we do and say is enough or is it good enough. We continue to feel undermined, misunderstood, and often mistreated. Sometimes by the very ones that are just like us, the female. We mastered being the victim and the victor simultaneously, and we have equally learned how to smile while crying inside. Not only are we the hidden figures, but we have hidden things that have yet to be unveiled.

As a Hidden Figure, we must force ourselves to push beyond the mundane of normalcy to a place of authenticity. Authenticity is the foundation of creative fulfillment. We lack dignity when our search for something more significant is constrained by societal, cultural, and traditional restraints. It leaves us feeling empty because we adapt to a set path that others impose on us instead of creating our authentic voice and journeys. It is not until we are willing to be vulnerable, flexible, and transmittable that we will have a relationship with our creative intent and legacy.

I don't ever remember being told that I had a purpose, or I was created to be an antidote to a global challenge, issue, or crisis that may exist. Instead, I was given a limit or category that society felt was reachable and attainable for who others perceived me to be. Usually, the types were secretary, receptionist, cashier, customer service representative, and depending on the day and times. They might have mentioned a teacher, doctor, lawyer, or librarian. Especially since I am a female being a Global Educator, International Panelist, Leadership Mentor, Special Adviser, Serial Entrepreneur, World Civility Ambassador, or possibly a Female Civility Icon, never entered their minds. If I am truthful, it never entered my mind either. I can't recall any of my teachers throughout the years ever saying that I should seek, search, and adventure out and find my purpose. But, I can clearly remember one of my male African American classmates, raising his hand to tell what he wanted to be when he grew up. He loudly and unashamedly said that "I want to be the president when I grow up." I will never forget the response that was given by our teacher. She said, "I don't believe that will ever happen for you." But as I write this forward, I want to declare to you that "You can, you will, and it is happening for you."

I can recall trying to be everything that everyone else wanted me to be. I always tried to please family, friends, church traditions, and perspectives of what everyone else should be. I never once stopped searching for myself and seeing what I truly desired for my life. I finally got to a point where I became exhausted mentally, physically, and emotionally. I thought the answer was similar to a fairy tale. Get a job, find a career, get married, have children, and happily ever after. But that is not how it works, and that is certainly not how it happened for me. I was the little girl who came from a divorced home that turned into a one-parent household, with a mother who struggled to keep food on the table and clothes on our backs. My sister and I never went hungry, but we didn't necessarily always eat what we wanted. We didn't have the name brand clothes and shoes. My mother made our clothes, and my sister and I shared shoes, coats, and anything else we had. My mother always taught us to be true to ourselves and that we could be anything we wanted to be. Still, sometimes the small-town environment, where everyone knew you, limited jobs, limited perspectives, and limitations in existence all around us, made everything seem impossible.

I tried a marriage that abruptly ended in divorce, shame, discouragement, and defeat. I was embarrassed, financially bankrupt, and it appeared that I might not ever recover. In reality, it took me years to recover. During the marriage and divorce process, I lost who I was, and I became unrecognizable even to myself. My confidence was at an all-time low, and defeat looked like a great victory for me. It wasn't until I got quiet and intentionally started developing my lost relationship with God that I finally found me again. I realized that it wasn't about the job, money, relationships, family, friends, or anything tangible or material. It was indeed about my spiritual, mental, emotional, psychological, physical, and alignment with God. That is when I was able to see His will for my life.

It took me a long time to figure out I was created with a purpose and for a purpose. Not that I wasn't wondering or looking for something different, but even more significantly, I knew of God, but I didn't always know Him. Once I indeed developed a relationship with God, I understood the need for vulnerability. I was vulnerable enough to allow God to control my life. Because of God, I am a creation that creates a Hidden Figure that shines bright for all the world to see. I had to agree with God, take control over my life, start listening, obeying Him, and not be afraid to be vulnerable to what was on the inside of me. Here are the steps that I took to do that, which ultimately led me closer to finding my purpose.

Being able to see is what is surface and limited. However, insight gives us an in-depth view of where we are at that present moment. We still need an enhancer with the ability to see, which provides us with precision and an undeviating channel to view things with a tunnel effect. Being able to see is what is surface and limited. However, insight gives us an in-depth view of where we are at that present moment. Our view will elevate as to increase keen radar. Visibility first examines the quality and condition of where we are. How we view our purpose, and to what extent or quality do we believe our purpose is to us and others. Visibility is not about the individual being seen but about what can be seen irrespective of your presence. Your visibility, seen or unseen, should penetrate an environment, atmosphere, and climate to give people an accurate understanding of purpose.

You don't have to announce or sell your purpose. Purpose alone will extend itself to those who are in need and to those it is intended to reach. You cannot expect to reach everyone, but you can anticipate lives being affected by your purpose. No matter how cold the world gets, allowing the warmth of ambition to be a coat of protection. Live in your purpose, as it was made suitable just for you. Your purpose will illuminate a conscious spiritual awareness and awakening from nonexistence to existence. You will not fully and wholly exist without your purpose, and your purpose will not exist absent of you. As a Hidden Figure, you have a purpose, meaning, and strategic intent. You are not invisible, and everything that you do is visible to God.

Prof. Ona C. Miller, EdD, PhD

Hidden Figures

Introduction

Dr Nadia Watson-Anthony, PhD

Introduction

Genesis 2:18-24 "Then the Lord God said, "It is not good for the man to be alone. I will make a helper who is right for him." From the ground God formed every wild animal and every bird in the sky, and he brought them to the man so the man could name them. Whatever the man called each living thing, that became its name. The man gave names to all the tame animals, to the birds in the sky, and to all the wild animals. But Adam did not find a helper that was right for him. So the Lord God caused the man to sleep very deeply, and while he was asleep, God removed one of the man's ribs. Then God closed up the man's skin at the place where he took the rib. The Lord God used the rib from the man to make a woman, and then he brought the woman to the man. And the man said, "Now, this is someone whose bones came from my bones, whose body came from my body. I will call her 'woman,' because she was taken out of man." So a man will leave his father and mother and be united with his wife, and the two will become one body.""

She is a HIDDEN figure….

When you think about books that make you have lingering thoughts long after you close the book, sometimes it's the characters that stay in your thoughts. Sometimes you can't stop thinking about the situation. — Unknown Author

"The Key to Extraordinary is a beautifully written, real life, love, experience and being celebrated for your hidden work. THF not only creates a delightful setting and has women that draw one in, but also adds a bit of empowerment, a push magic, and the unexpected to each bio storyline that makes this book a first of its kind even more enjoyable." —Dr Nadia Watson-Anthony.

"A virtuous woman isn't ruled by her passions-she passionately pursues an incomparable God."

"A woman's heart should be so hidden in God that a man has to seek Him just to find her."

"As a 'Godly Woman in Progress' are you choosing to keep your heart with all vigilance, realizing that from it flows the springs of life?" – Patricia Ennis"

"Nothing is more beautiful than a woman who is brave, strong, and emboldened because of who Christ is in her."

The Hidden Figures in this great history book have learned how to remove obstacles out of their way, each woman continues to strive to gain higher access. She dares to be "first" to break new ground, small gestures changed her life. The veiled figures used their privilege to empower other women to become better focusing on the upbuilding of the kingdom, all while allowing diversity to emerge naturally. **We are The Hidden Figures,** *"The 'Hidden Figures' Who Crunched*

Hidden Figures

The Numbers In Civility, Entrepreneurship philanthropy, Nonprofits and Authorship."

This book was inspired by Three brilliant African-American women at NASA -- Katherine Johnson (Taraji P. Henson), Dorothy Vaughan (Octavia Spencer) and Mary Jackson (Janelle Monáe) the women that served as the brains behind one of the greatest operations in history: "The launch of astronaut John Glenn (Glen Powell) into orbit, a stunning achievement that restored the nation's confidence, turned around the Space Race and galvanized the world."[Hidden Figure Wikipedia]

Just as HF has impacted the world THF has done the same but in a different way. THF women in this book served as the brains behind many great operations in history such as, communities, Households, Work, Health, Started a business, Wrote books, Built Programs, Served in Ministries and or a Trade.

As a whole, each section will acknowledge her existence and will grant her as astronaut of the year. Being invisible to the world, tucked away in her work she will be publicly rewarded, unveiled and exposed in broad but mostly satisfying terms.

Today we celebrate the few women who decided to write a book in the mist of the year 2020 pandemic Covid-19.

As a whole each woman believes in putting an end to

unsustainable folly and teaming up with other successful women across the globe!

Six POWER take home for readers

1. Life will eventually add up and pay you back
2. Everyone matters
3. Know the power of advocating for yourself
4. Embrace the power of a team
5. Remember the power of women advocating for women
6. Always leave a legacy for all women and girls

Kimberly Kupkake Kauffman, the WIFE FITNESS INSTRUCTOR that reached the stars of perfection in her BODY TRANSFORMATION contest while raising four children and still maintains a household.

Julian Businge, The Royal Branding Queen that has impacted nations.

Ona C. Miller, The DYNAMIC EDUCATOR that traveled throughout the world lighting the fire of all mankind CREATING the first of its kind GLOBAL LIBRARY OF WOMEN.

Tamika Harris, The EDUCATIONAL DIRECTOR AND SON-FLOWER MINISTRY FOUNDER helping women stay spiritually strong through conference and yearly events.

Tiffany Peters, The NURSE that took horseback

riding to another level.

Michelle Herbert, The FAMILY MISSIONARY

Michelle Frank, The NURSE PRACTITIONER that adopted a MEDI spa right in her clinic, helping locals stay healthy and confident.

Raine Diane, The LIFE COACH that gives "Raine REALITIES DAILY"

Althia Milton, The Fortune 500 MANAGER

Paula Emberling, The HIDDEN ADVOCATE

Siemone Anthony, The THREE-TIME AUTHOR that packed up and moved to the top of the world to explore what living was all about.

Enyonam Assoklou, Togo Africa's FRENCH MINISTRY LEADER

LaRonda Mills, The woman that took ENTREPRENEURSHIP to the next level.

Beatrice "BEA" The **CEO of Uniquely Bee**

Techima, The MISSIONARY that traveled spreading the gospel to all creation creating programs and human nutrition plans.

Jessica, The missionary and GRADUATE of TEXAS A&M COMMERCE, that Pursued her cosmetology license in order to help women view themselves differently.

During the process of writing "The Hidden figures" each woman experienced being a part of the global pandemic. Not a typical common cold, this killer of a cold was knocking down women and men across the globe. As Historical COVID records and great documentation we will include a timeline located in the back of the book.

Celebrating a HER-O

Each and every woman doesn't get the credit and worldwide recognition as she deserves. Seriously— women get left unrecognized which is why The Hidden Figures book is here to expose hidden work and talents of women across the globe.

Women's history has not been defined enough as a category of writing done by women.

"Though obviously this is true, many scholars find such a definition reductive."— unknown author.

What makes the history of diverse women writing so interesting?

Well, in many ways it is because we have been trained to be divided, judge outward appearance and use indicators of someone or something's value or worth.

Hidden Figures

During this lifetime I have discovered that, we cannot know what someone or something is like just by judging the color of one's skin. *"The quality or character of someone or something cannot be judged just by looking at them and an opinion of someone or something cannot be formed solely by seeing what's on the surface."*—Unknown Author

The tradition of women writing and women supporting women is where I would like to stay for a brief moment. Due to the inferior positions women have held in male-dominated societies. It is still unheard of to see diverse women writing history books and or anthologies.

My goal for this book was to create a women's biography, categorizing and creating an area of study for a group of people marginalized by geographic location and to explore through writing their lives as they are occupying such a unique sociopolitical space within their cultures.

Not surprisingly, many of these women will capture their hidden truth and become runaway bestsellers. Just like these women; Remember, Florence Nightingale the nurse that worked hard to change health care practices and saved many lives in the process. Today she is considered the mother of modern nursing. —Unknown Author

What about, the amazing true story of four, African-American female mathematicians at NASA who helped achieve some of the greatest moments in our space program. Not to mention the woman that combined her ancestors' passion for service with her own adventurous spirit and her belief that girls could do anything. [Juliette Gordon Low founded the Girl Scouts.]

What about Sonia Sotomayor? Before the Supreme Court Justice took her seat in our nation's highest court, she was just a little girl in the South Bronx.

Lastly, Fly girls, The remarkable, underreported history of the 1,100 Women Airforce Service Pilots aka the WASPs who served despite constant obstacles with determination.

I can go on all day about people throughout the world that have done amazing things.

But I know, you are probably thrilled because you are ready to see what your friend, daughter, mother, sister, granddaughter or co-worker has been up to.

While many of the authors have conversed and have focused on documented historical figures of other people but have never embraced the ellipses in history in their own lives. As each and every day goes by these THF workday and night in secret places to leave the world greatness.

Although they have not become household names yet, I leave them all with this encouragement. "Everyone   should   know   their incredible contributions to the world."-Unknown Author

Here are all the amazing women you should have heard of but probably haven't.

As an invitation to speculate on women's secret lives and untold stories, I would like to welcome you to the untold stories and first series of this great history book.

"THE HIDDEN FIGURES"

The Women Who Crunched The Numbers In Civility, Entrepreneurship philanthropy, Nonprofits and Authorship.

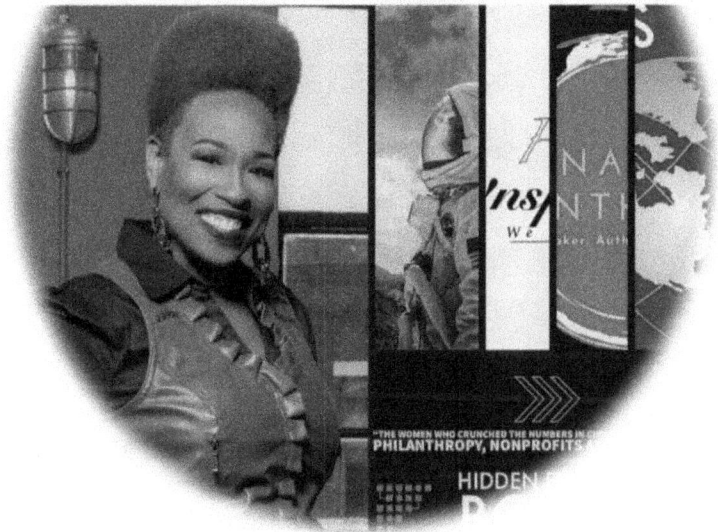

Professor Ona C. Miller

Author | Ambassador | Advisor | Advocate |
Female Civility | Panelist | Speaker

Professor Ona C. Miller is a Global Educator, Panelist and Humanitarian. In addition, she is an International Professor and the Founder of The Female Civility Initiative that is an international, intercultural, interracial, intergenerational initiative for females worldwide. The Female Civility Initiative has several subsidiaries, which are The Global Female Civility and Leadership Institute™, The Global Library of Female Authors, The Global Female Publishing Group, and Little AMAZONS. Professor Ona is the Female Civility Icon and Founder of "National Female Civility Day" which is celebrated every year on the 17th of September and is in conjunction with her Female Civility Global Initiative. She is a qualitative researcher that has extended previous studies in the secular universities but has expanded her expertise in the sacred faith-based universities as a strategic educator that searches to create an author curriculum to change the perception and position of Women globally. Professor Ona has an earned Doctorate of Professorship and an earned Doctorate degree in Organizational Leadership and her expertise is in "Resolving Issues by searching reasons of behaviors with Women as it pertains to Female Civility, Women in Leadership, Global Relations, and Organizational and Structural Leadership."

Professor Ona has over 20+ years of experience with the Department of Homeland Security (DHS). Her expertise and experience are in the fields of Finance/Accounting, Management, and Organizational Leadership. Her doctoral education has afforded the opportunity for her to examine ethical frameworks, principles, and practices of leadership. Additionally, Professor Ona understands the challenges dealing with change in strategic planning, cultural diversity, cultural behaviors, and global diversity. Her Master's degree in Management encompasses organizational communication, leading change, managing cross-cultural environments, social responsibility, project management, budget/finance, and business law. Her Bachelor's degree is inclusive of effective communication, innovation, statistics, decision-making, ethical/legal topics, and human resource management.

She has received a World Greatness Award and inducted into the World Book of Greatness as an Icon of Greatness with Greatness University in London, UK. Professor Ona served as a panelist on "The Role that Civility and Leadership in Social Protection at the United Nations Commission on the Status of Women (CSW63) and will serve again for (CSW64) sitting on a panel for conversations for a Peaceful and Inclusive Society.

Professor Ona has collected and continues to seek data to identify the internal and external barriers that exist for women because of social, economic, cultural, and traditional barriers, while implementing strategies for women to overcome.

Professor Ona was a Founding member on the Board of Directors for YOU! Empower a non-profit organization designed to provide disadvantaged women and families with the tools and resources to empower themselves towards a self-sustainable lifestyle.

Professor Ona is an advocate for women and an authorized Civility Spokesperson with the Civility Speakers Bureau and the author of motivations books, workbooks, and Case Studies to help women gain confidence, equality, advancement, and stability. Professor Ona has been awarded the Women of Global Solutions Award and the Golden Rule International Award by the iChange Nations™ Organization supported by the United Nations.

Professor Ona's mission is WombHER Foundation for antiabortion and anti-abandonment for women. Women must stop aborting and abandoning their purpose and identity. As the former National Economic Director and Legislative Adviser for the United States Women Christian Chamber of Commerce. Professor Ona provided a strategy to build, restore, and fortify women who are faith-based business owners.

Professor Ona has been awarded the CFO Award for Superior Mission Achievement Comptroller Award by the Department of Homeland Security. Professor Ona is passionate about education, empowerment, and leadership. She believes that to grow we must learn from the history of our past and implement new strategies, narratives, and disciplines to attain a better future.

As an author, I wrote several books titled #I Am Single, 8 Elements for Implementing Your Purpose, 8 Elements for Implementing Your Purpose Workbook, and Supplements for Life's Deficiencies, Christian Ministry Leaders: The Barriers that Women Face in Non-Profit Organizations, to help women be confident with who they are, to add balance to their lives while pushing beyond barriers.

Quick Facts

- Founder of Conori Consults, Inc.
- Founder of National Female Civility Day
- Founder of Womanhood
- Founder of Little AMAZONS
- Founder of The Global Female Civility and Leadership Institute
- Founder of Female Civility Initiative
- Founder of The Global Library of Female Authors · Featured in Voyage Magazine
- Featured in Power Woman Magazine
- Featured in BizFit Magazine
- Featured in The Jacksonville Progress
- Featured in The Times – NWI.com
- Featured in World Book of Greatness 2020
- Dissertation Content Expert, Grand Canyon University
- Founder of iPrenuse
- Founder of WombHER Foundation

Awards & Honors

- 2020 Icon of Greatness Award
- 2020 ICN Greatness Award
- 2019 World Civility Award, ICN
- 2019 DHS In-Service Award, Department of Homeland Security
- 2017 Exemplary Leadership Award
- 2017 Golden Rule International Award
- 2017 Women of Golden Rule Dialogue
- 2017 Women of Global Solutions
- 2010 Superior Mission Achievement, Department of Homeland Security
- 2010 CFO Comptroller Award, Department of Homeland Security

Author & Co-Author

- 8 Elements for Implementing Your Purpose.
- 8 Elements for Implementing Your Purpose Workbook
- Christian Ministry Leaders: The Barriers that Women Face in NonProfit Organizations.
- Supplements for Life's Deficiencies
- Female Civility in Leadership
- The Face of Civility
- Civility and Womanhood

Degrees & Certifications

- 2019 Doctorate of Professorship
- 2018 Global Ministry Certification

· 2017 ICN Statesman Certification
· 2017 Life Coaching Certification
· 2016 John Maxwell Certification
· 2016 Doctorate of Education
· 2012 Masters of Christian Studies
· 2011 Project Management Certification
· 2010 Masters of Management
· 2008 Bachelors of Science in Business
· 2007 Associates of Accounting
· 2005 Accounting Clerk Certification
· 2005 Accounting Technician Certification
· 2005 Accounting Assistant Certification

Professor Ona C. Miller's Organizations

- **Female Civility:** The goal is to build a bridge for Females globally to be able to make a greater impact. Females are designed to be sitting at the table and we will compete with anyone. Females are the missing piece that is vitally needed around the world for making the desired global impact. Our voice has the sound that resonates security, safety, and substance that the world desperately needs to hear. Our influence as females transcends division and promotes unity. A movement that educates females on how to be the best individual that they can be. Through education females will understand and maintain the perspective that they were created as a unique voice that the world must hear. We offer attributes of intuition, security, soundness, and substance.

The first step to education is identifying those key areas that are broken and breached, and then build a bridge for recovery.

- **Little AMAZONS:** Little AMAZONS was created and established to provide "Little Dresses" to Female Orphanages, Schools and Academies worldwide. The Female Civility Initiative - Little AMAZONS has been graced with the privilege of partnering with Goshwe Simi-Simji, Founder/Executive Director of Simji Girl-Child Empowerment Initiative & Orphanage/Simji Integrated Academy (SIA) - Nigeria. In the days, weeks and years to come we will continue to expand distribution in other countries and continents.

- **WombHER Foundation Womb HER:** Foundation is an anti-abortion and anti-abandonment critical mission that intentionally focuses on the elimination of abortion and abandonment physically, mentally, emotionally, and purposefully.

- **SHE Phoenix, FEMME Phoenix:** It's aimed at transforming the lives of pregnant youths and adolescent mothers, at advocating for their rights to a better life, at raising awareness about obstacles such as teenage pregnancy, sex trafficking, among other things.

- **YOU! Empower:** Founding member on the Board of Directors for YOU! Empower a non-profit organization designed to provide disadvantaged women and families with the tools and resources to empower themselves towards a self-sustainable lifestyle.

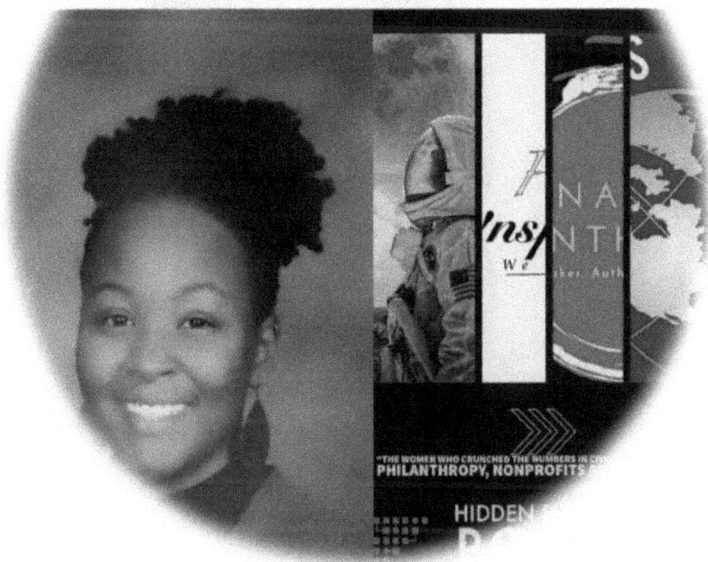

Meet

TECHIMA
DAVID
CO-AUTHOR

Techima David

Philanthropist, Authentic & Veracious

Where Her Feet Goes

When Techima David was born in the twin-island republic of Trinidad and Tobago nestled at the base of the Caribbean archipelago, she was given an opportunity to live with purpose. Did she know what that purpose was? No. Did she find that purpose? For that, she still lives. "And we know that all things work together for good to those that love God, to those who are called according to his purpose" Romans 8:28. For now, every past encounter, achievement, experience and qualification prepared her for the current profession in mission work and outreach ministry, which she is involved in today.

Growing up, Techima was an energetic child who needed to burn off the excess. At the tender age of six, she held her mother's hand as they entered a karate dojo to sign up for classes. Although intimidated, she felt that it was something she needed to conquer. She put on her Gi and her pristine-colored white belt and for the first time, she was immersed in the training of Shotokan karate. Every she set foot in that dojo to train, she felt her intimidation disappearing and a new sense of purpose replacing it. While learning values good character development, she also learned that the capacity to stand while others have fallen was not a privilege but an opportunity to lend a helping hand. She has won many competitions, however, she found herself wanting to help others rather than compete. This was the initiation of the moment Techima understood that there was more to life than receiving and winning. After obtaining her black belt at 12 years, she began to teach karate, which made her one of the youngest karate assistant instructors in the country. While training, she found herself teaching others to defend themselves and helping them to build that same character that was instilled in her. Subconsciously, she was learning what her purpose in this life was.

At 13 years, her feet walked from the dojo to run on the fresh grass of the soccer field as she was called to train as a goalkeeper for her country's national Women's soccer team. She trained 6 times a week; running, sweating, training. Even with her knee injury, she found the willpower, strength to continue her training. Her running eventually turned into flying which took her to Singapore to play soccer at the Inaugural Youth Olympics. Additionally, Techima's cultural experience was expanded as she traveled all over the world and in the Caribbean to represent her country, learning to be a cultural ambassador for her twin-island state. However, with her team's constant travels she missed a significant amount of school time. The discipline she developed as a child paid off as she spent her free time self-studying and attending after school classes for her regional examinations (Caribbean Secondary Education Certificate). Within this time, she learned to be driven, focused, and ambitious in excelling in everything she did while learning to represent what meant the most to her.

Hidden Figures

After 7 years in secondary school and ending her commitments with the national team. She set foot at the gates of the University of the West Indies, not knowing what she was going to do next nor what the future had in store for her. Nevertheless, she sat among the 3 walls and the whiteboard and pursued her bachelor's degree in Human Nutrition and Dietetics. She planted her feet among student representatives board for her faculty representing what meant the most to her- the unheard voices of students. With discipline in her studies, she became an awardee of the University of the West Indies Development and Endowment Fund Bursary and also the Head of Department Prize for Best Performance in Human Nutrition and Dietetics. Her feet took her back to the dojo, back to teaching karate to children. During this time, she also occasionally visited nursing homes and children's homes to spend time bringing joy to others.

Techima grew up in the Church of Christ with her family, she went to church religiously every Sunday and participated in any events they hosted. Was she on fire for God? No, but the summer after finishing university changed all of that. She spent one week as a guide for a young mission group from the Madison Church of Christ (Alabama) that visited Trinidad and Tobago in 2016. These advocates for Christ were beacons of pure joy, peace, and joy and represented something greater. She walked with them in the scorching heat daily to share God's message. For the first time, she ran into Christ and experienced a

33

burning desire for God's presence in her life. This experience aided her renewed love for Christ but simultaneously allowed her to discover her passion for missions and helping others to see the beauty of Jesus. Thereafter, she actively began seeking God's Word and searching for any opportunity to assist the community. Subsequently, she was certain that ministry was where God wanted to use her to bring people to Him and she was zealous to share the gospel and her testimony with those struggling in their faith. She was unraveling purpose in her life- Helping others

At 22 years, she flew to the dusty flatlands of Lubbock, Texas to enroll and begin her studies as a missionary apprentice with the Adventures in Missions program at Sunset International Bible Institute. As she studies biblical teachings, she also began working with a team at the Central Church of Christ in Tulia. There, she fostered relationships with many members of the church while sharing the Gospel with her team in the area. From the elderly members, she gained wisdom and from the younger ones, she regained her appreciation for the finer things in life. Although the youth group was a few kids, her team spent a lot of time teaching them, playing out in the graveled car park and taking them on service work the team had planned. She helped with Sunday school and even spent time with the Spanish congregation. She also served with a team at the church of Christ in Clovis New Mexico, where they helped with potlucks and volunteered at the local shelter. Often during her time in AIM, she took class trips that reached different states. She volunteered with the boys and girls club of Lubbock spending time with the kids in the after-school program. Her team helped in Houston after the Hurricane organizing food items at food banks, painting houses, helping clean neighborhoods of debris. She also spent time working with the Hope Beyond Bridges program distributing food, clothes and offering different services to the homeless. This program taught her to be a servant and to be flexible and grateful in every situation. Her purpose was becoming more concrete-serving others.

She said her goodbyes in Lubbock before leaving for her missionary internship in Mexico City, Mexico. Living in Mexico as a missionary allowed her the privilege to share God's Word. The facilitation of English classes to families in rural areas enabled her to obtain wider perspectives, and a more profound and all-round sense of humility. She found joy and purpose in building relationships. She further began spending time with families in the church and found her true calling in helping and mentoring teenage girls between battling with their faith to become effective, well-equipped disciples. She was able to use testimony to bring these girls together and which led her to develop a young women's support group to serve as a safe haven for them to share personal experiences and even create stronger bonds amongst themselves. She used her earlier years of Karate training to develop a six-month self-defense program for the children and teens of the church. Within the program, she gave nutritional advice, helped the kids develop character and opened conversations to share God. Occasionally, the team in Mexico took seven-hour trips to a small village in Mexico called San Luis Potosi. This was where she spent time cleaning the church there and singing, fellowshipping and giving out solar players to the villagers.

Having completed her time in Mexico and graduated from the AIM program in April 2020, she returned to her homeland, eager to get involved in ministry. In addition to maintaining her mentorship to these Mexican girls, she started working with the Venezuelan refugees teaching English and providing grocery boxes and clothing for them. However, with the existence of the Coronavirus, her country was experiencing some remnant of a lockdown and many of her students have been unable to access the internet to participate in her English classes. Nevertheless, she continues to deliver grocery boxes to them monthly and also to destitute families on the North Coast of Trinidad to remind them that God will provide despite all adversities. Simultaneously, she spends her free time pursuing an MBA in General Business Management with the University of Bedfordshire in the United Kingdom, so that in the future, she would be well-equipped to manage any ministry she is involved in and also pass her knowledge to others.

Although she is 25 years, she envisions herself to stay true to her purpose, helping and serving others, thus making her eager to remain in ministry long-term. She would love to continue doing international missions, specifically serving in Spanish-speaking countries to bring the gospel to the lost, just as she once was. Furthermore, her dream is to create a non-profit organization that provides support, mentorship and mediation for struggling teenage girls, young women and by extension, their families in the church.

"Whoever brings blessing will be enriched, and one who waters will himself be watered" Proverbs 11:25. True purpose comes in giving; giving of time, giving of patience, giving of joy, giving of service and giving of self. God will replenish and fill you with what you need and the fruits of your labor will come.

Hidden Figures

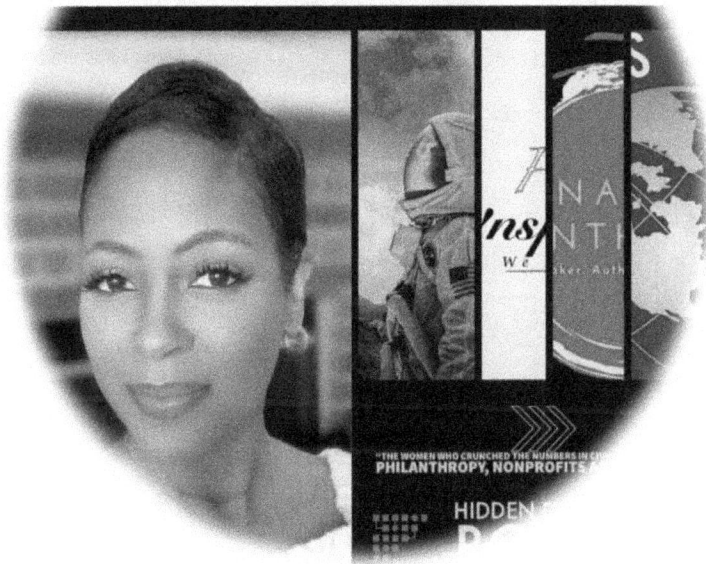

Meet

LARONDA
MILLS
CO-AUTHOR

LaRonda Mills

Ambitious, Compassionate & Intuitive

Fear not, for I have redeemed you; I have called you by name, you are mine. When you pass through the waters, I will be with you; When you walk through fire you will not be burned, and the flame shall not consume you. Isaiah 43: 1-2 ESV

These words of the prophet Isaiah do not promise us a way around, but away through. It's not a question of if you pass through waters that would threaten to overwhelm or walkthrough flames that would seek to consume you... it is simply a matter of when.

Redemption does not guarantee us safety in this world; it is a promise that we will never walk alone.

When LaRonda was a younger woman she did not understand this. LaRonda wanted to avoid confrontation, heartache and troubles at all cost. She was so thankful that God saw beyond her fears and saw the longings of her heart.

At the age of 18 LaRonda had her first child, at the age of 19 She became pregnant with child number two and life as She knew had most certainly changed. Her mother had always been a stay home mom and her father was the breadwinner of the family who suddenly passed away the same year that She was pregnant with her second child.

This was one of the most challenging points of her life. Here LaRonda was with one baby and another on the way and the man who had taken care of her; her whole life God called home. LaRonda's whole world was shook! Here she was with one child, another on the way and still basically a kid herself.

By God's Grace She pulled herself together, not only was now responsible for taking care of herself; She had two little ones depending on her as well. So LaRonda became a certified Nursing Assistant. The next few years things were going well, then BOOM at the age of 23 her mom suddenly passed away, just when she thought she couldn't feel any pain worse than losing her father. LaRonda's world was crushed! Her mom was her rock.

A life of consistency and stability-without fears and insecurity did not exist for her anymore. LaRonda's heart, mind and soul were searching for a place in life that did not exist. in spite of her best efforts, situations arose for her daily that made her uncomfortable. Of course there was a vision in her head of who she could become if she overcame her fears, but the vision was often blocked by the insecurities that filled her head.

Small challenges made LaRonda sweat and squirm. She could remember thinking if she could just get over this one thing, then everything else would be smooth sailing, but just like the waves on the ocean that one thing was always followed by another one.

"If voices of insecurity, If doubt, and fear are not confronted, they will dictate your life."

As years passed and life went on LaRonda continued being a Certified Nursing Assistant providing for what was two which now was 3 children as a single mother.

But of course LaRonda did not stay single for long. By the time her third child was almost a year old

She married her first husband. They had good times and bad times, but the bad outweighed the good so after 13 years of marriage they divorced.

So, there she went back into a shell, thinking she would not have to pass through the waters, still not understanding what Isaiah 43: 1-2 really meant.

"On the inside, learning to change and control the way we think about what we have faced does not come naturally. Even more challenging is having the heart to look forward to the future with optimism. In fact that takes great intentions, but what I have learned is that God does not promise us smooth sailing, it has been said that 'still waters run deep' but, that is only true for bodies of water that are defined to a certain space."—LaRonda

What helped LaRonda is when she changed her way of thinking and the same source that created the ocean and filled it with rhythm created her and she is unstoppable and powerful as the ocean.

LaRonda has been giving the gift of being on earth

for a reason. She writes, "Recognizing who you are and what you have to offer will help you realize that you do not have to be a slave to any preconceived idea of what your life must look like."

"There may be times when feeling this way really scares you, but remember we are fearfully and wonderfully made and God wants to give us the desires of our heart, but what are we willing to give him."

After being in health care over 25 years, not being as young as she used to be and on marriage number two. LaRonda started to explore other options for her career. As She prayed about it, it was pretty clear that at some point She would be going back to school to become a Licensed Esthetician and the thought of that alone was scary being in her 40's and seeking change, but not having the support from home was even more scary. So, the decision on going to school along with other issues led her to another divorce after being married for only 1year. So once again here come all those voices of doubt, fear, insecurities, saying things like "Don't do it! You can't handle what will come after this. It was days that She struggled to get out the bed and go and some days She didn't.

One morning LaRonda woke up at her daughter's house headed to the bathroom to find sticky's all over her mirror and to this day LaRonda's daughter doesn't realize how much she helped her mother out. Along with prayer, LaRonda's daily affirmations from her daughter and a great group of women from school who she now calls her "Esty Besties".

In March of 2016 LaRonda completed school and became a Licensed Esthetician, and Skincare Specialist.

Life just got a little bit easier.

From the start She already knew that she wanted to work for herself so, after graduating school and becoming an Esthetician, Skin-life By LaRonda was born. She wishes she could say that this was the smooth sailing part, but once again here come the waves with the flames.

When God closes a door, trust him. LaRonda ended up losing everything and moving in with her daughter and her husband. Can you imagine waking up one day feeling like everything is ok only to go to bed and realize what you thought life was going to be like was gone. Like it's said Man plans God laughs.

Message from Author LaRonda: "I remember going to one of my close friends crying on her floor and she began to pray for me and that's when I realized that I had been sidelined by God. During this time, I gave God everything I had and all that I was and it wasn't until then and only then that I started to receive what God had for me. First off, he gave me a husband that I wasn't even praying for, not only is he a good man but a Godly man as well... Yes, ladies there is a difference! We worship together, God is the center of both our lives, a husband who supports and prays for my vision and together we built Skin-life By Laronda, a home-based Spa that has been up and going for two years now. The vibrancy of your life is contingent on your ability to accept situations that isolated you and to learn and be empowered by your uniqueness. It's going to take work, and it's going to demand transparency and vulnerability. It might not feel safe, but you will be transformed into a better newer version of yourself.

You are blessed because you believed that the Lord would do what he said. Luke 1:45

Skin-life By LaRonda

Michelle Frank

CEO, Visionary & Advisor

Hidden Figures

Michelle Frank, MSN, APRN, CNP is a Child of God, a Mom to three beautiful daughters, a Health and Wellness Fanatic, an Entrepreneur, a Nurse Practitioner and the CEO of the following companies: Esprit Health & Wellness, LLC (est. 2014); Central MediSpa, LLC (est. 2016); Frankly Ours, LLC (est. 2016); and Esprit Body Sculpting, LLC (est. 2020) in Sidney, Montana. Her three daughters are her pride and joy: Breanna is a second class midshipman at the United States Merchant Marine Academy who excels in academics, leadership, and athletics. Her courage and bravery in leaving rural Montana for the East Coast and then serving in locations around the world on large ships is inspiring; Claire is a senior in high school and will graduate a semester early so she can pursue a dermatology internship. During the COVID-19 pandemic, she created a support group called Snacks and Chats, which is an anxiety and depression support group for teens. She is intelligent and driven, with her end goal of becoming a dermatologist similar to Dr. Pimple Popper; and Violet is a bright and talented fourth grader who loves to read and loves to dance, especially in the styles of musical theatre, jazz/lyrical, and hip hop. The family is completed with their 15-year-old shih-tzu named Eleanor.

Faith, family and community have always been integral parts of shaping Michelle's character. As the oldest of five, Michelle is blessed to be part of a loving, supportive family. She grew up on the family farm/ranch with wonderful parents, three sisters and a brother. All were active in sports, music, school and

community service clubs, church, and 4H. And all are highly competitive! She has been surrounded by an extended family of Aunts, Uncles, Cousins, Grandparents and Great-grandparents. In fact, when she was born, she had nine (9) Grand- and Great-grandparents! The farm/ranch life provided a foundation of family values, strong work ethic, and a good-neighbor mentality. The family is very close and has grown to include in-laws, nieces, nephews, and many dogs! Michelle has one Grandmother who is 94 years old. She is vibrant, witty and beautiful.

Michelle is a small-town girl who has stayed close to her roots. She is a single mom, divorced in 2019 after a 22-year marriage. She graduated from a close-knit high school class of 35, and treasures the lifelong friendships created from her childhood. After high school, Michelle attended the University of Mary in

Bismarck, ND, and completed 38 credits in two semesters. She then returned to eastern Montana and went to work at the hospital and clinic. Her career and varied experience in healthcare, including the medical and dental arenas, began in 1994. She worked as an admissions receptionist, a certified medical assistant in an internal medicine office, a clerk in the hospital business and insurance office, and also as a dental assistant, patient care coordinator, and dental hygiene coordinator.

Michelle was married in 1996. She continued to work and always had an entrepreneurial spirit, working in the direct selling industry representing Mary Kay cosmetics and PartyLite. She was successful in these endeavors, yet she always felt the desire to achieve more. She was motivated by her children and returned to college in 2004 when the distance learning program through Miles Community College (MCC) offered an associate of science degree in registered nursing. She became a certified nurse's assistant (CNA) and worked her way through school, gaining experience in Med-Surg and OB/Nursery.

While a student, Michelle was crowned Mrs. Sidney in 2005 and competed in and earned 1st Runner Up in the Mrs. Montana pageant. This was her one and only pageant experience, and pageantry was something she had always wanted to try. In 2006, Michelle graduated with honors from MCC and became a Registered Nurse (RN). Michelle's first job as an RN was on the Med-Surg floor at Sidney Health Center. She immediately continued her education and was accepted into the RN to BSN program at University of Mary. While working on that degree, Michelle enjoyed working in a variety of settings that rural health has to offer, and worked in the OR, perioperative care, same-day surgery, and home health and hospice.

In 2009, Michelle graduated with honors from University of Mary with her Bachelor of Science in Nursing and continued to work as an RN. She suffered a neck injury while caring for a dying patient that led to surgery, and she was no longer able to do the lifting involved in direct patient care. Since her goal had always been an advanced practice degree, Michelle pursued an opportunity with her alma mater, MCC, and became a Clinical Resource Registered Nurse. She taught and led students at two area critical access hospitals: Sidney Health Center and Glendive Medical Center. She was able to teach first and second year student nurses how to implement the nursing process while providing compassionate patient care. She also taught medical ethics as an online course. By year three as a nurse educator, Michelle had to make a decision on the Master's program track. She was accepted into a nurse educator master's degree program, but only days prior to starting withdrew and decided to pursue a Master's of Science in Nursing as a Family Nurse Practitioner. This offered more opportunity and choices: teaching remained a possibility, yet she could also care for her own patients and provide decision-making and support within her community. She taught at MCC and proudly watched three of her graduating classes cross the stage and become registered nurses.

In 2012, Michelle was accepted into University of Mary's blended Masters of Nursing - Family Nurse Practitioner program. She was also approached about a unique opportunity, and became the Nurse Manager and Clinician/ultra sonographer at Sunrise Women's Clinic, a pregnancy resource center. Michelle was instrumental in the transition of Sunrise Wellness from a pregnancy resource center into a medical clinic. She wrote policies and procedures, performed ultrasounds (after receiving the appropriate training and certification, of course) and patient care, and spoke at the annual banquet. Here she grew in her Christian faith while serving the community. She credits this experience with giving her the impetus to start her own clinic upon graduating with honors from the University of Mary's Masters of Nursing - Family Nurse Practitioner program in 2014.

The Benedictine Values and focus on servant leadership at the University of Mary strengthened her personhood. While her oldest daughter was at hockey camp in Minnesota, Michelle sat in the hotel room and wrote the business plan for her greatest endeavor. With a wide range of work experience and knowledge and a leap of faith, Esprit Health & Wellness, LLC, was established in June of 2014. Later that month, Michelle passed her boards and became an Advanced Practice Registered Nurse, Certified Nurse

Practitioner (ADRN, CNP). Esprit Health Clinic officially opened on December 1, 2014.

Michelle's publications and presentations include: Treating Dyslipidemia in Type 2 Diabetics (2015); Complex Regional Pain Syndrome and Vitamin C (2013); Conquering Obesity through Nutrition and Physical Activity (2013). In 2018, Michelle was recognized by her peers and the Sidney Chamber of Commerce and Agriculture as the Entrepreneur of the Year. In 2020, she is working on a book entitled, "Girl, Give Yourself Grace," with co-author, Dr. Nadia Anthony. Michelle speaks at various venues, including a Growing Up Gracefully presentation for school-aged girls and Health Promotion for her PEO Women's group. She is active at church and sings with the Praise Band. She formed and directed a women's choir, and also served as a confirmation youth leader.

Michelle values her personal relationship with Jesus and exemplifies a life of servant leadership and faith in God. She devotes time each day to read the Bible and has found the YouVersion Bible App to be a wonderful resource, especially in recent years during a very busy, stressful, and uncertain season of life. She has been through the struggles of entrepreneurship including a fallout with business partners, turnover of entire staff, rebuilding, and a contentious divorce ending in a two-day trial. She would not be who she is today or where she is at today without all the positive and negative circumstances, people, relationships and influences in her life thus far.

The mainstay, the constant, is her faith and personal relationship with Jesus. Her favorite Bible verse is Jeremiah 29:11. She wants to glorify God with her life, and you will often find her listening to music, singing with the worship team, sharing words of encouragement with family, friends, patients, and community members. She values the lessons in trying and failing, making mistakes and owning them, and then picking up the pieces and moving forward. Failing, after all, is the key to learning. There are so many moments in her life she has been in complete awe with the way God has uplifted, upheld and sustained her, her family, her business endeavors. God's grace has helped Michelle get through it all and become the person she is today, which is still a work in progress!

One thing she finds very encouraging is the fact that God is not finished working on her, or any of us, yet! She has only recently come to understand the importance of being a work in progress and has realized that one does not arrive and then simply coast through life. We are dynamic individuals and are always learning, growing, and changing, finding new ways to thrive and contribute to society as a whole.

Michelle understands the importance of hard work, persistence, and resilience. She is definitely a type A personality, very driven, with faults of perfectionism and people pleasing. To achieve balance, Michelle is an avid reader and especially enjoys books recommended by Focus on the Family and New Life

Ministries. In 2019, she attended a Finding Freedom workshop by New Life Ministries that helped her immensely in navigating a dark season of her life, helping her to emerge from a toxic relationship and find the bright spots of a very dark season of her life. She admires the works of John Maxwell, Brene Brown, Steve Arterburn of New Life Live and New Life Ministries, Annie F. Downs, Dr. David Clarke, and finds encouragement and solace in music by musicians of For King & Country, Danny Gokey, Lauren Daigle, and Mandisa, to name a few.

In the midst of a pandemic, mid2020, Michelle attended a "Dare to Lead" workshop based on the research of Brene Brown. She is invigorated and refueled by learning and leadership opportunities, and never has a shortage of continuing education credits related to maintaining her professional licensure. The challenges of shelter in place and quarantine related to the COVID-19 pandemic dampened Michelle's ability to seek out continuing education and growth while fostering a love of travel, yet have afforded new opportunities and different avenues to find community in learning. During this workshop, she took a deeper dive into her top two values of Integrity and Authenticity. Michelle's behaviors that support her number one value of integrity include choosing to do the next right thing, and modeling/being grounded in faith and Godly living. This does not mean she is blameless or without fault; it simply means she accepts God's gift of grace and begins each new day with a clean slate and a grateful heart.

Michelle's behaviors that support her number two value of authenticity revolve around being open, honest, reflective, and self-aware.

When a few of her closest friends were asked to help provide a spark and contribute to the biography, this is what they returned:

"This is about Michelle's life, but I will tell you, she is such a big part of mine. One very important characteristic I see in her is her unwavering loyalty. I went through turbulent times in my life and she was always there to listen. Never to judge, always to listen and show she cared! Just seeing her recently made me realize how at home she makes me feel. She has such an inviting soul. I can't help but smile ear to ear when I see her, and just giggle at the simple things in life." - DK

"I have been impressed by the way Michelle has been able to prioritize her life to represent where her beliefs come from and shine light on the faith that she has. She has taken leap after leap, trusting in God, and also in her ability to follow through and land on her feet. If you ask her, she'll humbly respond with something about how this or that could improve, but if you look for yourself, you'll see perfection and results that couldn't be achieved without dedication, precision, and attention to even the smallest details." -CJ

"Five years ago I needed a new Health Care Provider because my Dr had moved away and someone highly recommended Esprit. When I met Michelle, she was very warm, gentle, caring and reassuring to me she knew her field. After a few visits I realized she was driven, goal oriented, had lots of dreams and was passionate about her work. We definitely were on the same page in our approach to life: A-type! I liked that and soon we were sharing books, information and passions. Michelle has a genuine compassion for people and listens with her heart! When Michelle was going through some very difficult times, she was very good at seeking out counsel from those who can help and advise! She is a great listener and very teachable. Very humble in spirit! I can say she is a breath of fresh air in her search to understand and know Christ more. These last 5 years I have seen tremendous growth in her personhood and her desire to be all God gifted her to become! She puts a smile on my face and a gladness in my heart that she is so willing and wanting to be Christ-centered!" -DP

Michelle credits the people and relationships, both positive and negative, that have shaped her into who she is today. She is eternally grateful to her parents and immediate and extended family. She relies on God and understands that He cannot steer a parked car. We must keep moving forward in our own strength, accept His grace, and trust His guidance. Here are her tips on surviving and thriving during life's highs and lows, while not letting circumstances steal your joy:

How to have a great day everyday:

Bible app: Reflect, read, pray.

Journal: Acknowledge and record three (3) things to be grateful for.

Move that body: Physical activity/exercise 30+ minutes per day.

Nutrition: Choose nutrient dense foods, minimize sugar intake, and drink 8-10 glasses of water.

Vitamin supplements: NutriDyn for the win! Contact Michelle at Esprit for your personalized professional supplement prescription.

Community: Send a text, make a call, drop a card in the mail, stop by to visit those you love. Volunteer to serve at an organization that is in line with your values,

Rest: Get some sleep! 7-8 hours minimum.

Ask for help: This is difficult for type-A, entrepreneurial CEOs, yet it is important to recognize the need for help and tell those who love and support you that you need and appreciate them.

Choose joy: Smile, laugh, and surround yourself with people who uplift you and support your dreams. Hug your loved ones and tell them they are special. There will always be challenges and ups and downs we cannot control, but these simple actions, attitudes and routines can make a big difference!

In her spare time (haha), Michelle enjoys music, sports, travel, and reading. The year 2020 has put a damper on some of those, so she and her circle of family and friends have found creative ways to enjoy the beauty within Montana. She learned to kayak this summer and appreciates the Big Sky state. Michelle is always looking for ways to grow the business, expand her reach, and encourage and empower others.

Esprit Health Clinic & Central MediSpa offers an expert concierge experience for busy professionals which optimizes their health, wellness, and beauty goals. At Esprit, their mission is to promote vitality, confidence, and quality of life. Michelle and her team listen to understand personal health goals and priorities. New in 2020, Telehealth services and video visits are available to meet patients where they are. Ultimately, the personalized partnership between patient and provider is most important. Michelle and her team specialize in treating the whole person, and offer innovative treatments including hormone replacement, Botox and Juvederm fillers, weight management, professional supplements, skin rejuvenation with aesthetic lasers and chemical peels, body sculpting, wellness, and treatment of common health conditions.

The Values Statement on the wall in the waiting area represents the foundation of Esprit:

Educate and empower patients to take charge of their health;

Hidden Figures

Support therapeutic lifestyle changes;

Protect and provide preventive services;

Respect for persons with regard to autonomy;

Integrate local health and wellness resources;

Team approach to patient centered care.

Please visit www.esprithealthclinic.com for more information, or find us on Facebook via Esprit Health Clinic & Central MediSpa and IG via Instagram.com/esprithealthclinic. We have skin care and professional supplements to offer, and they can be shipped directly to your door! Cheers to your health!

Hidden Figures

Jessica Hayes

Honest & Loyal

Jessica Hayes is twenty- three years old and from Fort Worth, Texas. She is a new graduate from Texas A&M University in Commerce, Texas where she received her Bachelor's of Science in Learning and Technology. Starting in August 2021 she hopes to attend Sunset International Bible Institute acquiring her Bachelors in theology. She has also been a licensed cosmetologist for over six years and is driven by her passion for the beauty industry and educating others about it. She is continuing to build her portfolio and working on pursuing her dream of owning her own salon one day. Jessica is also a traveler. God has graced her with the opportunity to travel to places like Detroit, Michigan, Homestead and Key West Florida, Phoenix, Arizona, Stillwater, Oklahoma, Auburn, Alabama, Dubai, Lusaka, Zambia, and Seattle, Washington sharing the Gospel, connecting with other like-minded believers, and experiencing other cultures. The most impactful one of them all has been her trip to Lusaka, Zambia in Africa. She was blessed with the opportunity to receive the Hunter's Scholarship from the non- profit organization ARISE Africa and be in the presence of such an amazing culture and country. Their genuine love for the Lord and their encouraging faith Another one of her many accomplishments is becoming a co-author of a book called Women to Women where she had the pleasure of sharing her testimony of how she came to Christ. She finds great joy in sharing her faith and all God has done in her life. Philippians 1:6 – And I am sure of this that He who began a good work in you will bring it to completion at the day of Jesus Christ. What God has started He will finish. He has brought Jessica far in her faith and will continue to lead her. "The greatest glory in living lies not in never falling, but in rising every time we fall." - Nelson Mandela.

The people that have made the biggest impact on Jessica's life are not famous to the world but are known by God for sure. God has blessed her to cross paths with many people who have discipled her, encouraged her, and shown her true Christian living. Like her two college ministers and their wives Isaac and Heather McNally, and Luis and Huegette Carrasco, Jeff Smith founder of Discipletrips, Charles and Nadia Anthony, Jimitri and Ruby Green, The ARISE Africa and Zambian staff, and many others. These are the people who have been the greatest influences in Jessica's life. Giving her examples to look up to and follow as they follow Christ. 1 Corinthians 11:1- Imitate me, as I also imitate Christ.

As entrepreneurship as one of her top aspirations Jessica will be pursuing owning her own salon in the near future. Continuing her education in the cosmetology industry she hopes to receive her cosmetology instructor's license and one day open up her own school of cosmetology. Other future endeavors Jessica is excited for is starting her own YouTube channel with content that is fun, encouraging, and authentic. Authorship is something she will be continuing to pursue as well as working in ministry. Jessica's faith helps her to continue to persevere despite the hardships that come with pursuing her calling.

Hidden Figures

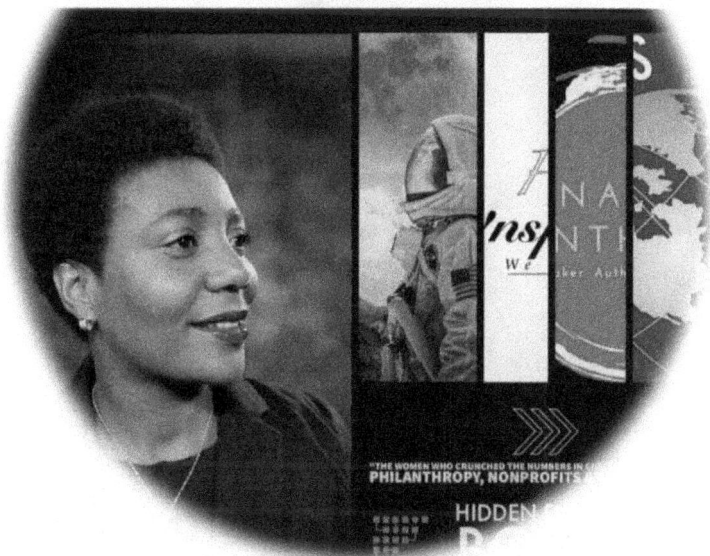

Meet

ENYONAM
ASSOKLOU
CO-AUTHOR

Enyonan Assoklou

French Africa Women Ministry

(F.A.W.M.)

One of the most needed mission fields in the world is the French speaking world especially the French African world.

My name is **Enyo Assoklou** I am a graduate of Sunset International Bible Institute (SIBI) with a bachelor degree in Theology. After my graduation, I headed to Togo West Africa where I organized the first Women retreat. We were 450 women participants without counting men and about 200 children. God has blessed our weekend growing in Christ by adding four (4) new souls to His Church.

By the way, I'm preparing the next Ladies days from the 26th to 28th of June 2020. I pray and hope that many more women and girls from all backgrounds will attend it because then, we will have more opportunity to share in love, the Good News of our Lord Jesus Christ with them.

I'm actually working as a missionary here in Togo with three (3) congregations. I have to travel often between three places: **Lomé** the capital of Togo, **Noepe** a small town about 35 min driving from Lomé, and **Bémé** a village about 3 hours driving from Lomé. I try to spend 2 or 3 weeks in each area. These last times I spend more time in Bémé the smallest congregation of the 3 because the needs are "**striking**"; first with the kids and, secondly with the ladies.

The joy of listening and learning the Word of God

Canvassing showing our love for Jesus. Inviting them to join us

One day was devoted for evangelization, and by the grace of God, the sins of four souls were forgiven by the Lord through the waters of baptism.

We all praising the Lord for the 4 Baptisms

Bémé Church Of Christ

Bémé is a small congregation in the Kplateau Région with beautiful members and wonderful children. They don't have a regular preacher because they have no means to support him financially. So Sunday, they receive one or two from Kpalime, a town about 25 km. They have to pay their transportation fees every single time. Though they face this kind of difficulty, from the beginning of the year, we already had three souls immersed in the waters of baptism; all praise is to God!

I'm helping the congregation with a children class. For the first time, children can learn at their level the Word. I have through Happy COC in Texas a few materials of teaching which I use to teach them. I didn't think I'm going to teach children but here I am, giving the best of myself training them from a small age to love the Lord and to walk at His path.

We are going to have in a few weeks a women meeting and learn together the place of a woman and her value at God's sight.

Every Sunday after worship, many of the members went out with the evangelists Daniel and Abraham to evangelize with hope to bring souls to the Lord. It is true that this help in different areas: fellowship, good deeds and of course financial resources. Three Sundays now, some of us walk to a village about 2 miles from Bémé to study with some people there where we have the three souls newly baptized I have mentioned before.

Twelve children at least attended my classes every Sunday and I enjoy serving them. We're studying Old Testament. The children adore learning through songs and art performances.

You can see them happily learning.

The Beloved brethren of Beme COC

I'm truly blessed to serve them particularly.

We at Sunday class with these wonderful little lambs

AMENOPE Church Of Christ

Amenope COC is situated at Lomé, the capital of Togo. Lome is about 126 Km. It means about 3 hours travel distance from Bémé. This congregation is much bigger than the first one but small compared to others. They're very interesting people in kind. I'm specially working with women there. They of course have wonderful children and more than 25 and they already have a very nice sister taking care of them. Of course I gave them the same material of teaching I am using with those in Bémé.

Can you imagine being in the midst of people even though they're brothers and sisters in Christ, and you couldn't understand their language or the worship on Sundays!

It is the case of Sister Dorothy who is from Ghana,

the neighbor country of Togo whose official language is English. She spent almost a year in the country after her wedding with a Togolese. But not knowing the language or understanding it, didn't help or encourage her spiritually. But since we've met, she enjoys worship with us because I'm translating for her each lesson and sermon; songs of worship and prayers. Her questions and answer at the Bible classes... The only negative part is that I have to work with other congregations and cannot be there every Sunday. I try to spend 2 or 3 three weeks in every town or village. I took it as one of my duties to serve her as I am there to help.

So every second Sunday, women gather together after worship and have special time in exhortations, fellowships or something spiritual to lift us up; that is my second duty in the congregation. We schedule in the coming days discussion as "women to women" where we can open up and share things that are needed to talk; a little bit like a therapy. I can tell you that, women face many problems in West Africa culture but one that become almost natural in people's mouth, but not in heart is "Polygamy". And some of our women live in Polygamy, have kids with their husband and are Christian... Also I just dream for our sisters to sit down and enjoy a time chatting with each other and see what can come out and then how to help. Yes, therapy!

The work is huge but unfortunately few workers in French Africa.

Second Sundays Ladies class at Amenope COC

With some children

Noepe Church of Christ

This congregation is situated in a very town where Catholicism is rooted. The difficulties are real in the way to break through their tradition into their heart. Many also practice voodoo even though they're fervent Catholics. How to touch their hearts? I praise God for the evangelist Selom Assoklou who is working hard there with certain patience I need to learn. His wife Georgette also is very patient and kind toward the population in general. They are very concerned by their problems and help in all they could to give them a helping hand. Brother Selom is always on the road to the bushes to evangelize and to plant churches. I forget to say also that he teaches in the Bible college of Noepe as the Principle. It was them who hosted the first ladies conference last June. And God willing the second edition will be there too.

This special conference brought together over four hundred participants from all places of Togo where the Churches of Christ are found. Because of its particularity, even the sisters in Christ on the other border, that is to say neighboring Ghana have honored it all together with those from the USA by their presence. As **Noepe COC** has no gathering place for all of us, **F.A.W.M** was obligated to build a temporary shelter for this five day meeting.

Building of the conference place

Me, Interpreting wonderful lessons given by Cynthia Evans (in the left) and Annette Williams (in the right).

The meeting place of the church in Noepe.

Preacher Selom, his wife and their 3 children

Hidden Figures

Meet

BEATRICE
LAMPKIN
CO-AUTHOR

Beatrice Lampkin

Entrepreneur, Industrious & Authentic

Envision a greater future, then become what you believe...

Beatrice "Bea" Lampkin, founder and CEO of Uniquely Bee, a women's fashion boutique, has always envisioned herself as an entrepreneur. Those closest to her have always been considered as hardworking, dedicated, reliable and "different." Different in a positive aspect. Different when it comes to her creativeness and her ability to think outside of the box.

For the most part, Bea was raised in a home with her mother, siblings, nieces and nephew. With her mother being divorced and having only one source of income to take care of the family, money was scarce. Her mother wasn't able to afford the life they'd been accustomed to because she was living check to check. However, as far as Bea was concerned, the wants for material things were still present. Part of the issue was that Bea felt entitled to these things because she was used to receiving gifts in return for her good grades. She felt since she was still making the grades that she should be compensated for them, even though her mother explained that things were going to be different when it came to anything that dealt with finances, it didn't completely sink in until after several heart to hearts. Once it did, Bea learned to mix and match her clothes to recreate new outfits. She also learned to be creative and rearrange furniture, as well as use things from around the house that she already owned to rejuvenate a space. Eventually she did extra chores around the house to make a few dollars to have for snacks or trinkets at school.

One year she sold candy for her elementary school's fundraiser and noticed how much money she made for the school. She wondered if she could do the same for herself. As a youth, Bea had a business mindset before she knew what it meant. She has many memories of ways she made money, but there is one particular memory that stands out from the rest. The one that changed the game for her. One summer, school was out for summer break. One of Bea's older siblings worked at a furniture store. The store would give out complimentary cookies and gourmet lollipops during store hours.

As the employees were closing the store, they would offer left-over cookies and candy to Bea and her younger sister. As children, they always accepted the offer. They would gather all of the lollipops that were collected throughout the week and go door to door to sell them. If they didn't meet their quota, they would wait for the company to stop by or take them to Wednesday night bible study to sell them. After they had made a profit, they would go to the grocery store to purchase a variety of candy to provide options for their customers. There were times when the money wasn't managed properly. They would scrape up change, purchase Kool-Aid and sugar, mix it together, put it in decorative sandwich bags and sell it. After the summer break was over, school started, then they were able to expand their business to their schools.

Growing into adulthood, the woman Bea thought she wanted to be, didn't have meaning nor value. It wouldn't have brought significance to anyone's life, especially hers. She thought she would be alone with a lot of money and expensive things. That was all to cover up the insecurities she had about her future. She soon realized she was too concerned with materialistic things rather than gaining spiritual knowledge or intellect. Foolish and miserable she would've been if that had been the path she pursued. It wasn't until Bea was a little older and had her first child when she realized her life should have more meaning.

As soon as she figured out she'd been going about her life the wrong way, her new mind frame overwhelmed her. She didn't know where to start because this would all be new to her. She evaluated her mother more and focused on how she was able to make sure everything was taken care of and how it made Bea feel about her. Bea wanted her daughter to admire the same way. She had the ability to create her own dreams. It was up to her to figure out what type of woman she wanted to be and focus on becoming that woman. Her thoughts were then, where does she start with limited resources. Where would she be if she started when she was younger? Starting so late in her years and now with a small child, she felt defeated before she started.

With no solid education, except for a high school

diploma, working a dead end job after a dead end job and barely making ends meet. Something had to give! Bea then started to reach out to community resources for assistance. One place would lead her to another, and she was starting to see improvement. She obtained her first apartment about an hour away from her hometown, but it was ok because she wasn't alone. Her older sister had an apartment in the same apartment complex, and they helped each other as much as they could. Through a temp service she found a job with the hospital that promised her a permanent position as long as she came to work on time and did her work.

Everything was falling into place for Bea just as she prayed for, until one day her car broke down. When that happened, she had to stay with her mother and leave her daughter with her sister. From her mother's house she would be closer to work but would have to ride the bus for transportation. This arrangement went on for a few months. She wasn't able to see her soon to be one-year old daughter and was close to missing her take her first steps. She despised the situation she was in and it took an emotional toll on her. She sent for her daughter and that just added fuel to Bea's motivation. She vowed to do everything in her power to provide for her and to make sure her baby had all that she needed. This included waking up at 4am, while it was dark outside, to catch the bus to make sure her baby got to daycare and she was due for work soon after. This also included being in the Texas heat for hours to make it back home in the evenings. She knew she had to move back to Fort Worth to progress. She reached out to the community again. This time the workforce solutions youth program. They were able to assist with childcare as well as provide funds for her education.

With no money saved, Bea had to plan for her move, her daughter's first birthday, and get ready to start school all at the same time with no transportation. She did not know how she was going to do it all. As always, she began to pray. This time a little harder and a little longer. As usual, God came through and Bea was blessed. She had a successful move. Her daughter had taken her first steps at her first birthday party which was celebrated a month after her actual birth month. Bea started school to be a Registered Dental Assistant then soon completed several months after. She believed since she had gotten her RDA, it would open doors for her and would obtain a job as a dental assistant. There would be room to grow in the dental field if she desired.

At the start of school, the students were led to believe they would more than likely have a job with the dentist they did their internships with. If not there, they would receive assistance for job placement. Unfortunately, things didn't happen that way for the majority of the students, including Bea. This was a huge disappointment, especially since she had quit her job at the hospital in order to finish school due to the workload and the schedule change. All she could do at this particular time is roll with the punches as her mother taught her.

Over the next few years, Bea worked for whatever company she could work for while she searched for a dental assistant position. She was turned down so many times. She was so desperate, she considered volunteering. Even though she had the proper credentials, she couldn't land a position anywhere because she didn't have experience. Every so often she felt like giving up. It seemed as if the more she tried to better herself and her situation, the more obstacles she had to overcome. Then she would get a burst of positivity. When that happened, she would take advantage of the energy and complete as many tasks as she could because she was able to think more rationally. This period was one of the most important times in her life. She was beginning to understand a lot of things, herself included. It seemed like there was test after test for Bea. At one point, she just went with the flow, because it felt like there was always a catch when she started to see improvement in her life. She was happy to be able to afford her bills at this point.

While Bea was bouncing around from employer to employer, she finally landed her first permanent job. It wasn't anything fancy, but to her, it meant stability. It was definitely different from her previous jobs. Bea was working as a customer service representative at a call center making $10 an hour. She was still having to stretch her income to make ends meet. When she thought about leaving, her employer offered an opportunity that she couldn't resist. The company offered to pay for their employees' health and life insurance licenses.

Upon completion of obtaining your license, they would then place you on an assignment as a licensed insurance agent paying $17 an hour plus bonuses. Bea took advantage of the opportunity and was able to obtain her license and work on the assignment as promised. This opportunity meant more than Bea understood at the time. She met new people on this assignment. A lot of them were older, more mature, and had experienced life.

Naturally, she met a few people and became close to them. They would all engage in deep conversations about real life situations. The more they conversed, the more Bea learned. Now the wheels in Bea's head started to spin again! All of the advice she'd received from her new friends, she applied it to her life and received new results. The more she opened up, the more she learned, the more her life was starting to make sense. She started to see things in a different perspective by listening and being open minded when speaking with people that were from different cultures and various backgrounds.

Bea loves to shop, always has. It doesn't necessarily have to be for herself. It can be anything from purchasing inventory, school supplies, to groceries, or even office supplies. What it is aggravating, is when she spends her hard-earned money on something, and the quality doesn't hold up for its price and terrible customer service. Whenever Bea experienced this, she felt taken advantage of. Customer service, if nothing else, should be a no brainer. One day, after expressing her disappointment amongst her peers, she decided that she should start her own boutique. This way she would be able to express her creativity, make another source of income, and offer the customer service she wishes to receive. She also noticed that most people love to shop for great quality items at an affordable price. Bea then gave birth to Uniquely Bee in 2017!

Mother's Day 2017, Bea and her husband took a huge risk and moved to Houston along with their three daughters. They literally dropped everything and started a new life. Nothing turned out as they planned, but everything is coming along perfectly. It wouldn't have happened if they had not stayed prayerful. This also shows growth in Bea's spirituality because she wasn't doing everything on her own. She learned to pray, listen for the answer, then move accordingly. She had always been hard on herself for not stabilizing her life in her earlier years, but having a family is what gave her some clarity. As she is figuring out what she wants to be, she is able to realize what she doesn't want to be.

Even during the COVID-19 pandemic, Bea has been extremely blessed. She is grateful to have been working as an essential employee for a fortune 500 company. A company that believes in their employees enough to pay their college tuition. In the middle of going to school for dental hygiene. All of the dentist offices closed down due to the pandemic. She learned there is no such thing as job stability and has decided to do what makes her happiest. There have been a lot of twists and turns just for Bea to combine all of her passions and make it into her life's work.

Bea believes that everything happens for a reason. Her plans did not happen when she wanted them to because she used her talents unfavorably by being selfish and greedy, but she now understands that she is able to use her gifts and talents in a positive aspect, to become more of an asset and to empower others. As trends progress, Bea will be able to apply her creativeness where she sees fit. After working on herself, a lot of praying and validation, Bea views her business differently. She feels as if she sees Uniquely Bee for the first time and is in the process of relaunching and rebuilding it.

Hidden Figures

Meet

ALTHIA MILTON
CO-AUTHOR

"THE WOMEN WHO CRUNCHED THE NUMBERS IN
PHILANTHROPY, NONPROFITS A

HIDDEN

Althia Milton

Resilient, Resourceful & Reliable

"The Manager that leads customers to healing"

Althia Milton, is a graduate of Mineral Wells High School as well as Weatherford College where she obtained a medical assistant license. She also at one point had an EKG license, always having dreams of helping others in some form or fashion or even just to make people smile has always been her goal. When Althia was younger her dream was to be a famous singer because She loves music, Althia believes that music has a way of healing people in some sort of fashion. Over the years Althia careers have taken many twists and turns which ultimately led her to Walmart.

During the pandemic COVID-19; FORTUNE announced the 66th FORTUNE 500, its annual list of the largest corporations in the United States, ranked by revenue for the 2019 fiscal year with Walmart being the top!

Althia Milton started working at Walmart in 2015 in the optical division, it wasn't her first time working in an optical office so she felt comfortable doing it again.

Althia has been with this Fortune 500 company for more than five years now and at this point with a company she loves to manage.

Althia found herself years ago switching jobs frequently but told herself, while still trying to find her way home, It was time for a change.

In 2017 while still living in Fort Worth Althia was diagnosed with multiple sclerosis. She didn't know much about multiple sclerosis except for the fact that she had an uncle who had passed away from it. Althia was very scared at the time, she had a four-year-old daughter and was a single mother living in the city and I did not know what the future had in store for her.

Around this time Althia lost her ability to walk, so she had to fight to gain to walk again.

Althia comments during her interview. "I remember laying in the hospital bed when a friend came to visit me and she told me 'it was okay to be sad even to be a little upset, but not to stay in that state of mind for long."

Althia was in a deep state of depression, at that time because she just didn't understand why she was going through this.

Althia found herself asking God "why me" In the end she found herself saying, "why not me"

I'm no different than anyone going through changes in their life, that is when the healing process began for me—Althia Milton

At this time Althia had to pack up the life that she knew and move back home with her mother. in Mineral Wells, the one place that she said that, she would never go back to.

BUT GOD!

God had other plans in store for Althia.

While working at Walmart Althia met a lot of people who have become her great friends. They aren't just co-workers, they are customers. Because of HER personality and how she is with people, Althia has been blessed to use her spiritual gifts in order to meet people who either have family members or spouses that have multiple sclerosis.

Althia has been advising families on how to deal with doctor's appointments and things of that nature and in regards to getting help with their conditions.

Surprisingly, overtime people would come into Walmart to thank Althia for helping them when they couldn't get help from anyone else.

Althia is making a difference in someone's life. "I have come to realize that sometimes you find your calling in the most unusual places."—Althia Milton

Althia is currently enrolling back into Weatherford College to pursue her Nursing career as an RN.

Althia leaves us with a message: "I am looking Forward to this new journey in my life and as long as God allows me to see another day, I'm going to use it to the best of my ability. not only for me but for my children and grandchildren as well."—Althia Milton

Hidden Figures

Meet

TAMIKA
HARRIS
CO-AUTHOR

Tamika Harris

Early Childhood Leader, Founder and Director of Sonflower to Sonflower Inc, Mentor, Adviser and Coach

Tamika Pope Harris is an experienced Early Childhood leader, Founder and Director of Sonflower to Sonflower Inc., Mentor, Adviser, and Coach. However, the most important title she esteems is wife, mother, and aunt. Tamika is a notably compassionate person, who is intentional with her interactions with everyone. She is selfless in her actions towards others. She has an infectious personality that attracts people to her. She is a people's person. Tamika is an impactful Woman of God that sees the best in all situations. Her transparency about her life experiences has been a saving grace to many. Although painful and embarrassing she has developed a skin covering that allows her to expose her truth and protect her present. She is a great listener and has the ability to skillfully filter when communicating with others to provide effective feedback to offer the best outcomes. As a coach, mentor and adviser she believes that transparency is essential to providing support to others. Overall, Tamika is impressively astonishing both personally and professionally.

She is a boy mom of 3 and loves every minute of it. There is never a dull moment with these 3 around. Life has a way of throwing some pretty hard blows. Tamika has had her share of life blows. Her love for her boys was a driving force to keep going, even when she wanted to throw in the towel. Tamika and her two older boys created a powerful relationship that evolved into a paramount unbelievable greatest relationship with the addition of her youngest son.

This mother son relationship wasn't easy but was worth every single distraction and hurdle. Tamika was intentional about having meaningful, supportive, healthy, and strong relationships with her boys that extends beyond the titles on the birth certificate. There was a time in her life when she was a single mother with limited resources and support. Nevertheless, she was driven by her goals and desires to provide an enhanced life for her children. Her source of refuge and recovery is her boys. She has also played an immense role in her nieces and nephews' life as well. Tamika desires for her nieces and nephew mirrors that of her boys. She wants the absolute best for them and works just as hard to ensure their lives are fulfilled. She loves them and they love their Nene.

Tamika has twenty-five years of experience cultivating strong relationships within the early childhood community. Her Early Childhood experience includes Pre-K, Collab PPCD/ECSE, Head Start, and Early Head Start. She is an accomplished leader holding positions as an Education Manager, Director of a Head Start program, as well as a Birth to Five Early Childhood Lead Consultant and Coach. She displays Flexibility with the educational landscape, culture and challenges across diverse districts both large and small. She accommodates and modifies approaches to meet the needs of each district and staff personnel. She does this by effectively communicating goals, so everyone understands expectations. She empowers team members using a coaching approach to use their talents optimally. She models productivity and quality standards. She is a true motivator that inspires everyone to do his or her best. She strives for a professional relationship with her team that embraces respect, accountability, and responsibility. As an early childhood leader, she has high expectations that promote learning and provide intellectual stimulation for teachers and herself. Her focus is that students and teachers receive opportunities that maximize learning and establish lasting relationships shaping a positive culture for progression. She focuses on strengths and applies minimal concentration on weaknesses. She values each person for what they bring to the team. She maintains current information about trends in Early Childhood. She creates positive environments that systematically incorporate a positive impact for all involved. As a life-long learner, she has positioned herself to learn from her others as they learn from her. As an effective leader she has created a safe learning environment that has high expectations for everyone to take full advantage of opportunities for their personal and professional growth. She does all this while maintaining high morale and a positive work environment. Her aspiration for the success of those she serves stretches beyond her career as an educator. Tamika has a heart for people, especially women. Her passion for women ministry, influenced the formation of Sonflower to Sonflower Inc.

The mission statement for Sonflower to Sonflower is: Where the impetus growth is intentional for each radiant flower to shine and glow up. Throughout her day-to-day interactions she can be found uplifting, encouraging, empowering and supporting one of her sisters. Tamika is a servant and a leader. She is fulfilled when assisting one of her sisters in their endeavors. She believes that behind every successful woman is an alliance of other women who encourages and supports her. When you shine I shine, When you win I win. When you Succeed I Succeed, I am you. She started this ministry to be a shining light into the lives of other women. It is vital and imperative to the mission of Sonflower to Sonflower, that we fix our sisters crown. Fixing her crown is for both of us. When I fix my sisters crown mines are automatically adjusted as well. Let's GLOW together.

As the founder and director of Sonflower to Sonflower, she is committed to being a luminous light to women all over the world. Women from all walks of life will learn to embrace their inner and outer beauty by transparency, honesty, and in reality. We are great just the way we are. Let's GLOW together. Sonflower to Sonflower is a Christian ministry for women, where women build each other up to succeed in all aspects of life. Everyone has a story, and life experiences. She believes that transparency of life is a remedy of support, which refreshes and energizes when imparted into another. Through Sonflower to Sonflower sisterhood is established as well as affiliations that opens up opportunities to collaborate and network as you GLOW. That radiant glow shines vividly inside and out. Through these powerful interactions, there is spiritual and personal growth that occurs, as well as a boost in self-esteem. As growth occurs, vision is also keen. The keen vision gives each woman insight into her self-worth and her true value becoming a "BETTER YOU". Sonflower to Sonflower empowers women to embrace reality of self. What you see is perfect and good enough and you deserve the absolute BEST. We celebrate each other, we encourage each other, and we love each other. We are Sonflowers.

Sonflower to Sonflower strengthens women in their individuality, restoring self-esteem, balancing ego, spiritual leadership, compassion, and wisdom through the word of God. In (John 10:10) it says, "I am come that they might have life, and that they might have it more abundantly". The women are empowered with the teachings of true faith and loyalty to something much bigger and brighter than they are. The women are empowered to love, one another teaching them to live in faith and not fear. (2 Tim 1:7) "God didn't give us a spirit of fear, but of power and of love, and a sound mind". This ministry displays that we as women are more than conquerors. (Rom 8:37)" Let's GLOW together. This ministry gave birth to a phenomenal women's empowerment conference and retreat.

She inundated her heart in women ministry from a yearning in her life for sisterhood. She wanted a sister to call, hang out with, laugh and talk with and even to cry with. Well God granted her that through her job as a consultant when she was assigned to support a teacher in Royse City, Texas. God blessed her with an older sister, her void was finally filled. This relationship lasted on earth for 10 years, and now she holds memories in her heart. Tamika has giddy moments when she hears a soft voice motivating and pushing her to keep going. In the name of sisterhood, and her favorite holiday the annual highly anticipated, My Favorite Things Christmas party was created. Tamika would like to take the credit for the party idea, but she found it on Pinterest. She has hosted this party with the assistance of her mother, "the cook" for the past 7 years. Each year the party has been an amazing event that leaves the ladies looking forward to the next party. COVID has stopped large gatherings, but COVID didn't stop the 2020 Favorite Things Party. The party is virtual this year. Aretha was the life of this party; she will forever be celebrated at the party. In Aretha's honor Tamika gives an additional gift to each lady. Aretha will always be remembered and celebrated in anything Tamika does. She loves and misses her big sister Ree.

In 2006 Tamika organized her first women's event, which was a prayer brunch. There were 10 ladies present including Tamika. As a supervisor on her job, it required her to meet with her employees the majority of which were women. During these meetings Tamika would facilitate and scaffold to conclude with positive resolutions that were empowering for the ladies. She wanted every encounter to be powerful and purposeful. She realized that people valued her knowledge and frequently would seek advice from her both professional and personal. Tamika felt that to be more effective she had to open up about her truth. Tamika was the speaker at the prayer brunch, she shared an intimate conversation regarding her life experiences. This moment of transparency when speaking at the prayer brunch was the freedom that catapulted inauguration of the Sonflower to Sonflower Empowerment Women's Conference. Ten years later in August 2016 was the first Sonflower Conference. Tamika and a team of committed individuals worked tirelessly to make the conference a success. It was a life changing conference for all in attendance. In 2017 Tamika and her team planned and delivered another powerful life changing experience. In addition to the committee Tamika's entire family worked alongside her to ensure the conference is successful. Tamika wasn't sure if this would be a recurring event. So much so that in 2018 she took a hiatus. However, she started to receive testimonies of how people were delivered, set free, chains were broken, prayers answered, and relationships restored during the conference. These testimonies were the momentum to revive what was started.

The Sonflower to Sonflower Empowerment Conference is an annual event that happens in the month of August. Since its inception the conference has been a day event. However, this event has evolved into a weekend of spiritual restoration. The conference will offer women of all ages an impactful, inspirational, interactive, motivational and empowering life changing encounter. The women will be able to connect and network with each other to build spiritual capacity. The women will leave encouraged and equipped to faithfully and completely use their Godly gifts to magnify the Lord. Sisterhood will be strengthened. The woman will learn the importance of fixing her sister's crown. There will be a jam-packed weekend filled with powerful praise and worship led by Tamika's husband and Music Director for the Conference. There will be preaching and teaching of God's word. There will be food, fun, fellowship, and love. This is all done in a serene ambiance that will allow the women permission to relax and focus on themselves, while absorbing invigorated knowledge to mature in their relationship with God. The prayer when planning this event is that everyone involved is empowered for greatness. Sonflower to Sonflower Conference is where the Empowered, Empowers.

Tamika's contact information is:

Email: tamikapope@sonflowertosonflower.org.
Facebook: sonflowertosonflower
Website: sonflowertosonflower.org
Instagram: @sonflowertosonflower
Twitter: stosonflower

Meet
JULIAN
BUSINGE
CO- AUTHOR

Professor Julian Businge

Founder of Royal Civility Global Initiative, Speaker, Property Coach, Author, and Royal Fashions Expert

'I am a Royalty Speaker and mentor helping people find their true identity through The Word of God.'

And

"I am a Property business coach and offer mentoring and coaching services to women looking for time and financial freedom".

About Professor Julian Businge

Julian Businge is a successful entrepreneur. She is the Founder and CEO of Royal Civility Global Initiative, a firm that specialises in helping people Discover, Develop, Deliver and Celebrate their true identity through the word of God of who they truly are.

She and her husband are co-founders of several businesses, e.g, Peace Apartments, providing serviced accommodation commonly known as Airbnb. Through this firm, she also offers mentoring and coaching services to women looking for time and financial freedom. Also Together with her husband co-founded World Greatness Awards.

Julian Businge is a Royal Fashions Expert who is creative, caring and customer focused. Her current project in 2019 has been working closely with the Queen Mother of Tooro and King Oyo, in Uganda to create unique Royal fashions and designs. This is aimed at blending tradition and modernity and creates modern-day cultural wear. She is a published author,

Award winning speaker, co-authored many books about, Royalty, property and business and is well versed in both areas.

She has been privileged to be coached and mentored by the great legends of our generation like Les Brown, the World's Number 1 Motivational Speaker and His Excellency Sir. Clyde Rivers, Ambassador at Large for Burundi and Founder of IChange Nations. With their help and support, Julian has gone on to become an inspirational speaker whose message touches people in all areas of their lives. She has spoken for various conferences and has won a speaker's Award. After listening to her message, one of her fans commented, 'It is because of you I did not give up on life'. She continues to work with people who are seeking to change their life's trajectory and rewrite their future. Indeed, Julian Businge is an example of a selfless humanitarian who is focused on helping people around the world achieve maximum success and live their best life.

Achievements

- Founder of Royal Civility Global Initiative
- Aug 2020 Honorary Professor of Royal Civility, UGCSI
- 2020 World Civility Ambassador
- 2017 Speaker /Author / coach
- 2019 Radio presenter
- 2019 Royal fashion expert

- 2019 Co – founder of world Greatness Awards
- 2017 Co- Founder of Peace Apartments
- 2019 Honorary Doctorate, UGCSI
- 2020 Great Britain Businesswoman of the year
- 2020 UN representative for the Peace society of Kenya
- 2020 Global library of Female Authors

Social Media Links

- https://www.royalbranding.org/
- Email : joliejasi@gmail.com
- https://www.linkedin.com/in/dr-julian-businge-8b06b236/?originalSubdomain=uk
- https://www.facebook.com/JulianMpanja/
- https://www.youtube.com/channel/UClh7m N6uhizV0E2FV6e9BVA/

Hidden Figures

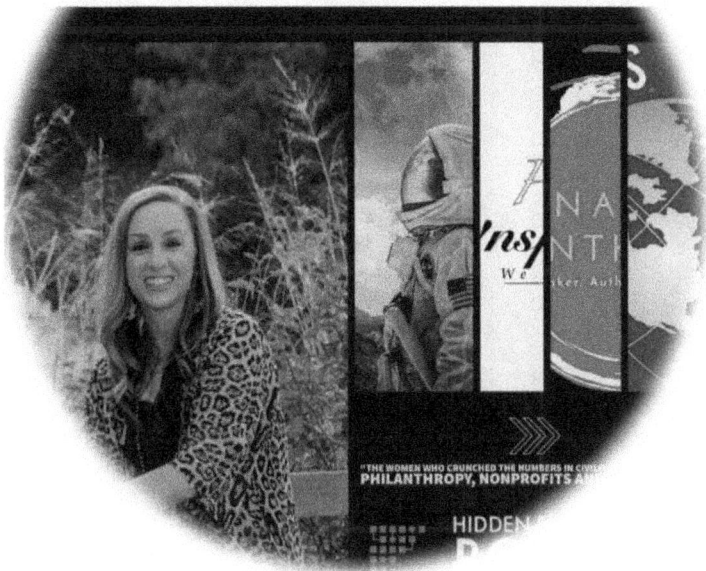

Meet

TIFFANY PETERS
CO-AUTHOR

Tiffany M Peters

Strong, Loyal & Honest

Tiffany was born a warrior in Midland, Texas on the first day of Winter in 1981. She had a difficult and broken childhood and moved frequently as a young child as her parents were in the racehorse industry. Her parents divorced and Tiffany, along with two younger siblings, were exposed to the effects of alcoholism and abuse throughout her mother's several marriages. At the age of 12, Tiffany was presented with the opportunity to work for a traveling dog groomer in her small town during the Summer. It was during this time that she developed the skills of the dog grooming trade. She continued grooming her friends and family member's dogs after moving from Spearman, Texas to Seminole, Texas.

In the 8th grade she was introduced to church, a youth group and Jesus by close school friends and eventually gave her life to Christ and was baptized. Tiffany was married at the age of 17 and earned her GED at the age of 18 after dropping out of high school. She and her husband welcomed a beautiful, healthy baby girl in June of 2000. Tiffany owned her own dog grooming business for several years before her daughter was old enough to start school. In the early 2000s, Tiffany had the opportunity to obtain her EMT-Basic and volunteered for a small-town ambulance company. This began her love of medicine and of people.

When her husband received an offer to work in Lubbock, Texas they picked up their small family and moved the hour and a half to the big West Texas city.

2009 began a two-year mission to earn her EMT-Paramedic certification. She graduated first in her class in 2012 and was awarded the distinguished Fred Hagedorn award, for having the highest GPA in her class. Tiffany's Paramedic certification led her to work for a privately owned ambulance company, in jail medicine, as a physician substitute and in occupational medicine.

In 2016 Tiffany began the LVN nursing program at South Plains College. She graduated with honors, Phi Theta Kappa, in 2017. Again, first in her class, receiving several awards including Student's Choice and Highest GPA. Her first job out of nursing school was at Texas Tech Health Science Center working in Orthopedic Surgery for Dr. Mimi Zumwalt, a Sports Medicine Orthopedic Surgeon. Tragically in December of 2017 Tiffany's little brother, Charlie, took his own life, changing her outlook on life and mental health forever. Although she dearly loved the physician, nurses, and staff she worked with, after 2 years in a clinic she was ready to live her dream of working in the hospital. Tiffany was offered a job at University Medical Center on the Geriatric Trauma Unit. Caring for geriatric patients and their families came as second nature for Tiffany. Palliative care patients were her favorite. Nothing compares to being able to share the love and comfort of Jesus with the families losing a loved one. It was an amazing experience that she will never forget. Tiffany is currently working as an infusion nurse at a busy Rheumatology Clinic located in Lubbock, Texas and is working towards her Critical Care Paramedic Certification and LVN to RN bridge program.

In addition to her professional life, Tiffany is also an accomplished horse trainer and barrel racer. She also breeds and shows Silkie chickens.

She and her husband, Adolf, are also involved in their church, The Worship Center. They serve on The Heart of the Matter Ministry and Relentless Student Ministry. She and her husband have been married for 21 years. Their daughter, Ashlinn (20), is currently attending Texas Tech University working towards her goal of becoming a psychiatrist.

Tiffany gives all of the glory of her success to God. She knows that He has plucked her from the fire many times and that she should be a statistic according to the world. A couple of her favorite bible verses are listed below:

These hard times are small potatoes compared to the coming good times; the lavish celebration prepared for us 2 Corinthians 4: 17-18

Glory to God, who is able to do far beyond all that we could ask or imagine by His power at work within us Ephesians 3:20

Achievements and Awards

- State of Texas Board of Nursing- Graduate LVN License (August of 2017)
- State of Texas- Paramedic License
- AHA CPR, PALS & ACLS
- FEMA Fundamentals of Emergency Management
- Difficult Airway Management
- Member of Phi Theta Kappa National Honor Society
- 2011 Dr. Fred Hagedorn Outstanding Achievement for Highest Consistent GPA
- 2011 Paramedic Class President
- 2012 Octapharma New Employee of the Year
- 2017 Outstanding GPA for Highest Consistent GPA
- 2017 Student Choice Award

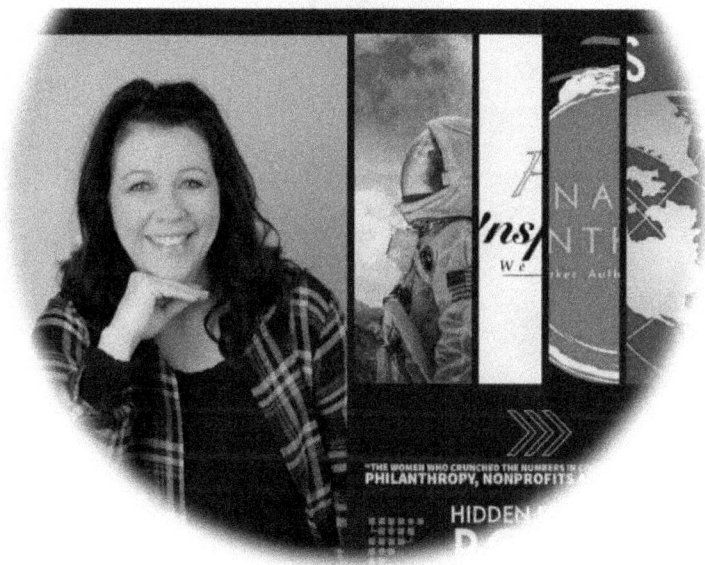

Meet

PAULA
EBERLING
CO-AUTHOR

Paula Eberling

Social Justice Advocate, Author & Speaker

Paula was born in Washington and moved to Montana at the age of three. She is a wife, mother, and grandmother. Paula is a social justice advocate, author, speaker, trainer, trauma support specialist, certified mediator, grant writer, and a survivor and leader in the movement to end modern-day slavery and human trafficking. Paula has served as the Director of the Seventh Judicial Victim Witness Program for Eleven years and has 22+yrs experience as a victim's advocate, humanitarian, and human rights activist. She passionately advocates for the services, resources, awareness, and social reform of victims' rights. Paula's influence has sparked state-wide participation as she coordinates multidisciplinary community response teams to create a cohesive response and support system for victims of crime.

Paula's journey began when she became a victim at the young age of three. She witnessed her mother's physical abuse and experienced abuse from her biological father and, in later years, the abuse of her stepdad. Her environment taught her how to become the perfect "silent victim." She became a master at developing coping mechanisms that allowed her to survive the sexual, physical, and psychological abuse.

Between the ages of twelve and fourteen, Paula was again sexually abused. After disclosing her abuse, she was humiliated, embarrassed, and blamed for her victimization. She became a runaway and found refuge in the streets, sleeping in the park, couch surfing, and homeless shelters. Her escape soon made her an easy target for sex trafficking. Her experience left her feeling used, empty and led to multiple suicide attempts. Eventually, she was arrested as a runaway and placed in the foster care system. At the age of fourteen, Paula became educated on the criminal justice system. She had been a victim of crime, witnessed a crime, and became all too familiar with the lack of recognition for victims' rights within the criminal justice system.

During the criminal process for the prosecution of her abuser, she realized that there had been many opportunities for authority figures, law enforcement, and social workers to learn of her abuse throughout the years. Paula realized authorities lacked the training to recognize signs of sexual abuse and trafficking. She knew that the lack of knowledge prolonged her victimization. At fourteen, the court denied permission to attend the sentencing hearing for her abuser. She was devastated, angry and demanded to participate in the hearing. When questioned by the Judge as to why he should allow her to attend, Paula informed the Judge that the very reason everyone was there was due to her victimization. She told the court that she needed to hear him plead guilty, and she had the right to attend. Listening to her abuser admit his crimes against her validated the crime and empowered her voice. She became an advocate for herself and would later advocate for others like her.

Paula continued to live in foster care until she was

sixteen years old until the system released her as a ward of the state. Looking to escape the public eye and scrutiny of her abuser's family and friends, Paula married at seventeen. She thought she was fleeing her past and starting her life over. She married at the age of 17. Paula found herself back into the all too familiar world of domestic violence. She stayed in the marriage for 18 years and eventually divorced. After her divorce, Paula moved to another part of the state. She worked in Economic Development for two years and later left to be the Seventh Judicial Victim Witness Program Director. Her years of being a victim had prepared her for her role as the director, but even more so for the advocate's position. When she read the job description, Paula knew she had found her calling.

The position has been a natural fit for Paula. She knew the familiarity of being a victim. She knew the importance of witnesses of crime, and she knew the criminal justice system. Paula found herself at home in her new career. She became an expert at identifying the needs of victims. Her years of experience made her an expert in her field. After years of service, Paula realized that the justice system was flawed, broken, and hadn't changed since she had navigated it. Paula became an avid advocate for others. During her years of service, she realized the importance of educating her peers, Judges, attorneys, and prosecutors. Giving victims a voice was not an easy task but supporting victims' rights was a priority.

Years of abuse and pain took their toll on Paula. She was timid, nervous, and quick to say yes when it came to working. She soon found herself subjected to sexual harassment in the workplace. Initially, her love for her work prevented her from reporting. Memories of her past experiences instilled fear reveal the harassment. She had been conditioned to be compliant and made it challenging to report her harassment. After being accepted into a state Leadership program and later a Master's class, Paula's classmates and facilitator reminded her to be the powerhouse that she was. She learned that being her most authentic self was her superpower. She discovered that she wasn't any less of a person because of her trauma. By embracing her truth, dismissing the shame and guilt, she found peace and purpose. Eventually, Paula reported the harassment and advocated for herself and others in the workplace, and brought change through new protocols for reporting harassment.

Working in the system gave her insight into the gap in services for victims of crime. She started a virtual support group for women of trauma, a free tele-med for teen victims of sexual assault, and is the founder of a human trafficking task force in eastern Montana. Her own domestic violence experiences prompted her to become a certified mediator to provide pro-bono services to victims of domestic violence during divorce proceedings and parenting plans. Paula learned how to write grants to fund program services. Additionally, she learned leading by example.

Through her healing experience, she has become a whistle-blower/ change maker of the justice system and the voice for empowering survivors worldwide. Her experience on both sides makes her an excellent liaison, bridging the gap between victim and advocate. In her talks, she openly shares her healing journey and professional observation of the loopholes that are ready to be filled in the justice system. As a survivor of domestic violence, a teen runaway, homeless, trafficking, child sexual abuse, psychological abuse, and sexual assault, she shares her stories of trauma and triumphs in her recently published book, hoping to instill hope in her sister survivors. Paula believes that your trauma can be your greatest strength, and you get to write the ending to your story.

To connect with Paula:

- pneberling@gmail.com
- peberling@richland.org
- www.paulaeberling.com
- https://www.facebook.com/lovinglife2day/
- Survive To Thrive, https://www.facebook.com/groups/4006826 74166684
- https://www.facebook.com/7th-Judicial-VictimWitness-Program-778009192241096
- https://www.facebook.com/Eastern-Montana-Human-Trafficking-Task-Force-115958256478158

Hidden Figures

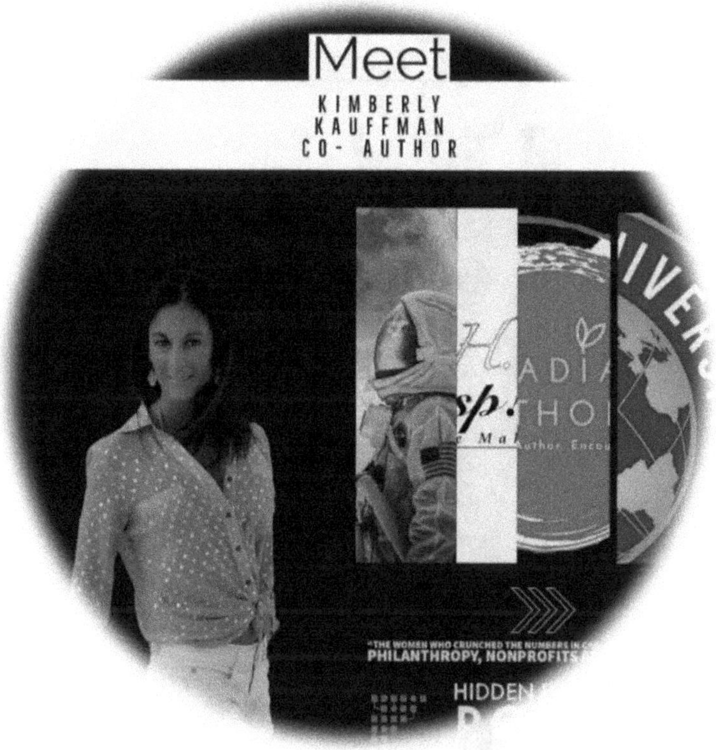

Meet
KIMBERLY
KAUFFMAN
CO- AUTHOR

Kimberly Kauffman

Beautiful, Dedicated & Honest

We all wonder what we will be when we grow up, for some it happens early in life and others it takes time to define and mold who and what we are. Our interests change over time and we discover through life experiences, what our passion is, our calling from a soft voice inside that nudges us to step out on faith and trust God with the gifts he gave us. This is the biography of how one woman found her passion, her calling to help others have, "Goals for Life."

On October 14, 1972, Jerry and Barbara Slaght welcomed their second child, Kimberly Kay. Kimberly has an older sister, Jennifer, and a younger brother, Robert. Growing up as a child, Kimberly was always using her imagination, playing restaurant in her room for hours, pretending to be a mother to her dolls and dressing up her dog, whom she had from kindergarten until graduating from high school. Mox was his name, named after her Grandmother, Katherine's dog. Many summers were spent traveling to their grandparent's home in Baker, MT, the town where her Grandpa, Dr. Weeks had been the doctor. Memories of the three-story house, playing in the attic with the full-size skeleton in the corner, riding the old bike with the banana seat to Ben Franklin to get a lunch sack full of candy for 25 cents! The best part was Grandma Katherine putting us in her basket on her three-wheeled bike and riding out of town to the oil well pads along the highway. Other memories with grandparents, Chleo and Francis Slaght, were eating breakfast at the B & B restaurant with her dad and siblings.

Kimberly's family also enjoyed many summers traveling to ghost towns, state parks, camping and swimming at Echo Lake. She could be seen taking her dog Mox in the rowboat and swimming with her siblings. One summer, her parents decided to put a pool in the backyard. Every summer thereafter was spent swimming in that pool, diving for rings at the bottom and her brother playing shark, which usually led to chasing her out of the pool!

During the winter the family did cross country skiing in Glacier Park, ice skating at Foy's Lake and sledding with her siblings that ended with having her mother's homemade hot chocolate with marshmallows! Kimberly also spent many winters downhill skiing on Big Mountain with family and friends.

Since the family lived out of the city limits, Kimberly would ride her bike a lot to get into town. The ride was downhill that turned into a straight stretch of highway for over a mile. On the way back home, the last quarter of a mile was uphill! Kimberly was up for the challenge and always pushed herself to ride up the hill in first gear on her 10-speed bike, dreaming of one day being in the Tour de France. Kimberly was also active with basketball and track.

Kimberly has always had a love of music. Her family would listen to the top 100 songs on the radio every weekend. Her and her siblings would stand on the fireplace hearth and use the fire poker as a microphone, dreaming of being on stage and singing while playing the music on a record player. To this day, she still has all the 33 and 45 records. As a teenager, Kimberly would use $10.00 from each paycheck to buy a cassette tape of her favorite group. Over time she managed to fill up an 18-gallon tote of cassette tapes.

Kimberly took many years of piano lessons and when the time came to learn an instrument, she chose the French horn. She played the French horn from 5th through 12th grade. Hard work and practice paid off learning to play the French horn with a trigger thumb. When Kimberly was a sophomore in high school, Paris, France was getting ready to celebrate their Bicentennial and was reaching out to as many states that would travel and participate as a high school marching band in their celebration parade. This would lead to Kimberly's first adventure traveling across the sea to many foreign countries without her family.

During her junior year of high school, she fell in love with her high school sweetheart, Joe Kauffman. They meet by divine intervention! Kimberly was having a rough day, she came into the band room where she was an aid for the teacher, and unannounced to her, so was her true love, Joe. When she entered the band room, she was stopped by a soft, hearted, caring guy who asked her if "she needed a hug?" The high school sweethearts married a year after high school and have recently celebrated 28 years of marriage.

Also, during her high school year, she had the opportunity to take a Certified Nurses Aide class that gave her a job working at a nursing home. She enjoyed all the aspects of working with the elderly. Her favorite part was working on the Alzheimer wing assisting residence with their quality of life.

The couple lived their first seven years in a mobile home, making ends meet, going to college at Flathead Valley Community College and living to watch Saturday Night Live on the weekends! After Kimberly earned her Associates of Arts Degree in Human Services, she used those skills and worked for a non-profit organization called Flathead Council for Families. She helped manage the front desk, handed out parenting information, and organized their yearly fundraiser.

After a few years of working for the non-profit agency, Kimberly decided it was time for a career change. She accepted a secretarial position at an OB/GYN office. Working at this office was a great experience from a medical view and gave Kimberly and her husband great insight of things yet to come.

During their first 10 years of marriage, Kim and her husband enjoyed hunting (Joe taught Kim how to shoot her first riffle, hunt for deer, and take care of dressing out the animal). Many weekends spent rock climbing with their dog Maverick. This was an excellent way to conquer her fear of heights! The couple also enjoyed downhill skiing at Big Mountain, camping, mountain bike riding and traveling to Butte to see Kimberly's parents. One of their biggest adventures with their dog Maverick was hiking to the top of the Great Northern Mountain located in the Flathead Range and Great Bear Wilderness, near Hungry Horse, MT.

In 1998, the couple was ready to buy their first home. They found a great home in a subdivision called Happy Valley. Lots of trees, and a state park close by to walk Maverick. After about a year in this home, they decided it was time for another dog, Maggie.

In 2002, the couple decided to start their family and welcomed their first child, Josiah David. Kim always wanted an even number of children. In 2004, Amberly Joe was born, 2006 Hannah Rosalyn and 2008 Teagan Kaylee. All four children were home births under the close care of two wonderful midwives.

The Kauffman kids were homeschooled by Kimberly until moving to Eastern Montana where they all attended a private, Christian school. Josiah earned his blackbelt in Tae Kwon Do and played many years of baseball. Amber played high school volleyball, Hannah and her love for animals, and Teagan being their gymnast. Plus, all three girls learned piano.

During the couple's first few years of starting to raise a family, there came an amazing opportunity to travel to Egypt and Israel with their church. They were gone for two weeks on a biblical route of Old and New Testament history. This journey through the Bible started in Cairo, Egypt to view the amazing pyramids, the Sphinx and the Cairo Museum. Some of her most memorable moment in Israel were riding a camel up Mount Sanai to watch the sunrise where Moses received the 10 Commandments, the High Priest Caiaphas's place where Jesus was beaten, tortured and held there until his crucifixion, and being re-baptized with her husband in the Jordan River. Before returning home, the couple would be expecting Hannah, their third child.

Along with starting a family brought the excitement of their new land surveying business, Big Sky Surveying, PC. This was a huge step for her husband and became a team effort to make the business successful. Kimberly assisted with payroll, taxes, and invoicing while her husband focused on the client's projects and field work. This was truly a family business; Joe would locate landmarks and Kim running the survey instrument with a child in a backpack!

Family has always been important to Kimberly. In 2006, her mom was diagnosed with breast cancer. During this time, Kimberly, who was pregnant with their third child, made several trips to help her mom with doctors' appointments and sat with her dad while her mom had surgery. Kimberly's mom is a survivor of breast cancer and enjoying life cancer free.

In 2008, her dad's health was not the best. He was suffering from internal bleeding and his body could not keep up while trying to make new red blood cells. Kimberly was pregnant with their fourth child during her father's medical struggles. Unfortunately, he passed away while she was still pregnant. Kimberly felt a strong desire to speak at her dad's funeral and highlighted some of his characteristics. He always had a funny one liner to say and enjoyed his country music. His famous words were, "I am glad you got to see me again!"

In 2010, there was a major change in the economy that greatly affected Kimberly's family. A mutual decision was made to uproot the Kauffman family and move to Eastern Montana to start life over. This transition began a new chapter, with many new beginnings.

Moving across Montana was not a quick transition. While Western Montana was in an economic crisis, Eastern Montana was flourishing with the oil boom. Rentals were almost nonexistent, and hard to come by. The family could not move all together, so Kimberly's husband took their class C RV motorhome and moved to Sidney, MT first. Living in the motor home filled with every piece of land surveying equipment he owned, Joe set the way for the family to soon be together. Back home, Kimberly began to pack up their newly built home. This was a bittersweet moment because the home was built to raise their children and enjoy family and social gatherings. One of the hardest things to leave in this home was a mosaic masterpiece that Kimberly had designed from their trip to Israel, the 5 loaves of bread and three fish. Kimberly told Joe that "she would go anywhere with him, family is where we are together, and making memories at the dining room table." Eventually, the couple made Eastern Montana their home and bought a house.

After moving to Eastern Montana, Kimberly was approached by a friend to run for Mrs. Montana. The thought of any kind of pageant was stomach wrenching as this was not her style. After giving it some time to consider, she made the decision to represent Sidney, MT in the Mrs. Montana Pageant. She was voted by her peers as Mrs. Congeniality, most kids, married the longest, winning the swimsuit contest, and placing runner up in the pageant. Kimberly never regretted running for Mrs. Montana. She gained confidence while the family supported her as she conquered her fears.

From this experience, it sparked Kimberly's interest in bodybuilding. She hired a personal trainer and began her 6-year journey of competing at the NPC level in the bikini division. Many hours, weeks, and months was spent eating, sleeping, and training for competitions, all while still helping her husband manage their business and raising their family. Some of the key components to her competing was her husband. Joe would help her master stage routines, spray her tan for stage, and help her find the right competition suit.

Kimberly's love, passion, and dedication for bodybuilding took her and her husband on competition adventures to Las Vegas, NV, Los Angeles, CA, Fargo, ND, and Missoula, MT. Finally, her hard work and dedication took her to Pittsburgh, PA for nationals where she placed top 10 in the bikini master's group. Today, all her trophies, crowns and medals from competing are proudly displayed in their gym.

During her years of competing, she studied and specialized in sports nutrition through International Sports Science Association (ISSA). Her desire for nutrition and weight training lead her to achieve an Elite Trainers Certification through ISSA that specializes in personal training, bodybuilding, nutrition, and sports nutrition. She also achieved through Precision Nutrition, a Level 1 certification in the Essentials of Sports and Exercise Nutrition.

Kimberly had a desire to take her knowledge and help other people by educating them with their nutritional needs and training clients at the local gym to be more confident and knowledgeable. One by one, through word of mouth, clients found her and began their own personal fitness journey. Kimberly teaches a boot camp class, coach's clients for better nutrition habits and weight training. Her desire grew to have a private gym to train clients that did not have a local gym membership or feel comfortable at a gym. So, in April of 2020, with the help of her husband, they were able to convert their garage into a private gym and purchase the necessary equipment to train clients. Kimberly has many years of weight training, nutritional, and professional knowledge that she loves to share. Her husband creatively came up with her alias name-Fitkupkake. You can search Fitkupkake at Fitkupkake.com, Instagram- Fitkupkake, and Facebook- Fitkupkake and Kimberly Kauffman.

Kimberly is thought of by her clients as determined and fiercely loyal, kind hearted, 100% genuine, no matter what, true to you, a great friend and powerhouse in the gym, the nicest person you will meet, inviting with a radiating presence. A beautiful person inside and out, very positive and strives for her goals. A positive influence on many people and a great mentor at helping men and women accomplish their physical and nutrition goals.

Kimberly's children think of their mom as strong, annoying, busy, but still loving, healthy, motivated, and good with people.

Kimberly's husband would describe her as the love of his life, committed, fighter, nonjudgmental, kind hearted, and trustworthy.

Nowadays you will find Kimberly up every morning at 5:00 AM teaching her Boot Camp Class, training clients, helping to get kids ready for school and always enjoying a cup of coffee with her husband. After that,

Kimberly will be back at the gym to help her clients achieve their goals.

In closing, when Kimberly was in her competition years, her mind set was "You can never get back a missed day of training." She made every day count knowing she gave it 100%. Make an improvement to yourself today, "Goals for Life!" Ready? 5, 4, 3, 2, 1!

Hidden Figures

Siemone Anthony

Author, Entrepreneur & Visionary

Siemone's career started when she went to a local college and developed a passion for Communications Once she graduated with an Associates in Communications she did not stop there. She then started her career as a communications specialist working in Security with Government. She obtained a top secret clearance working at the front desk as a receptionist and later being trained as a contractor for Raytheon Professional service and L3 Communication, overseeing the Labs and Security over AirCraft & Simulations information and documentations and she holds a certification as a Six Sigma Black belt

After 7 years in this field Siemone left Raytheon and started working as a self-employed contractor for Bradley D's cleaning services. I know this sounds a lot different from what you already heard but don't be fooled by the career change.

Working as a contractor opened doors to self employment and an adventure into her Entrepreneurship. During this time she was able to learn all about the cleaning business and what it means intellectually by traveling all over Texas doing new construction cleaning, for new or remodeled apartments, schools and hotels. This gave Siemone the insight she needed to successfully become a part of Dallas Black Owned Business owners Association.

Siemone used this knowledge and started contracting with homeowners that require the attention of housekeeping.

25 years later she still has the same clients who she faithfully services.

From there, she aimed to meet and exceed her potential, taking on new challenges and exceeding her own expectations.

Siemone changed careers and shifted to being at home more. At that time, she had 3 teenage daughters and some just out of high school that required much of the attention as a single mother.

The time at home led her to a career change but landed her right back in the skill set she adored, Communications.

Siemone accepted a position in Hotel hospitality, She was hired as a front desk clerk for Marriott International. Believe it or not she started off as front desk clerk for a brand-new hotel that was not yet opened when she started her and several others helped create the brand and get the hotel up and running. Once Siemone was working for two weeks she was asked to be the Front desk supervisor, but she knew nothing about this industry she took on that responsibility. This option gave her unforgettable life experiences. In less than 1 year she was approached by her manager and asked if she would like to be an Assistant General manager, which she greatly accepted. This the greatest opportunity that changed her life.

Siemone continued in this course of action by persevering. She trained countless pours to learn all she could about the hotel industry she took several classes and then went to a local college to get her Associates in Hospitality

Over 10 years in Hospitality Training & Development as a leader in Training

Co-Chair for Diversity for one of the Top 5 Hotels in Hospitality

Coaching and managing leaders for escalation in the Hotel hospitality industry

After being pushed in several different ways and being out in unfortunate situations, that left her almost homeless Siemone left the hospitality industry and decided to make some career changes.

Siemone went into the career that would give her the knowledge she needed to help not only her family but friends and others in need. She started working for the Mortgage industry. You see once you have lost a home and you've seen your loved ones go through Foreclosures and bankruptcies due to lack of knowledge and lack of financial planning, Siemone dove into the industry as if she knew all there was to know. But the point is she wanted to do all that she could to help others that had the same experiences she had by losing her home. Siemone started working for one of the top 5 Mortgagors in the industry. She started as a dispatcher, trying to get Homeowners to refinance their home loans and after 1 year she was forced to either apply for a different department internally or take a severance pay and move on.

The determination to keep her foot in the door to learn about the challenges of Mortgage, showed her that this was only the beginning. So, she applied within the company and received the position of a Debt counselor. Siemone is an expert at what she does. She is a top performer that exceeds the expectations of her role.

In this field Siemone has achieved her goals by using the knowledge to offer Financial Guidance to homeowners all over the United States

Siemone's certifications consist of RESPA, Fair lending training. Diversity, Mortgage escalations, Preventative financial counseling

As a Mentor, Coach, financial debt counselor, certified in Ethics and diversity and Business Owners of Siemone's cleaning Services: the Serving Dallas /Fort Worth TX area

Author and Co-author and Inspirational Speaker and Mentor

With Great expectations and with Excellent measure

I leave with you

"If you ever have the thought to end all that has come upon you, stop for a moment and ponder what you can actually do. Reach beyond measure and expect the unexpected. Make Greatness your ultimate goal

As with Greatness we become strong and develop a desire to exceed our own expectations Perseverance is the key. Strive for the best and think the unthinkable Let go of the past and embrace your future. The excellence in you will give you the ability to Rise. Share all that you can; know that your future is in your hands and your life depends on YOU

Jeremiah 29:11

For I know the plans I have for you"; declares the Lord, plans to Prosper you and not to harm you plans to give you hope and a future"

Be Brave

Siemone's Cleaning Services, Author, Co Author of Women to Women Anthology, H.E.R Inspiration.

Instagram: Siemone Anthony.
Facebook: Siemone Anthony
siemoneant@yahoo.com
Saartis129@gmail.com

Hidden Figures

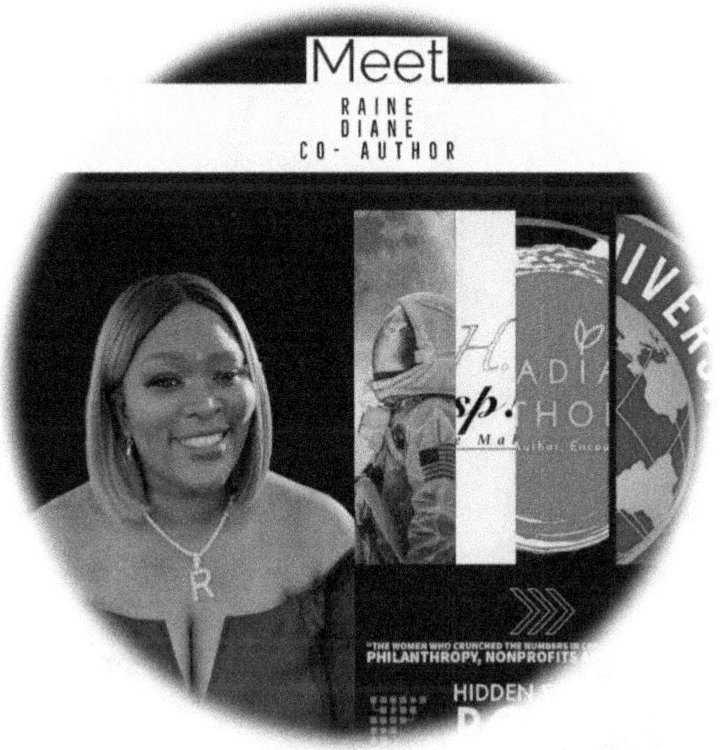

Meet
RAINE
DIANE
CO-AUTHOR

Raine Diane Fossett

Author, Coach & Visionary

Who is Raine? That is what most people call her anyway, Raine is a pretty unique name. It is a great conversation starter; it draws in attention. Raine Diane Fossett born Lorraine Diane Williams, that is her name but that doesn't answer the question about who she is. To some she may be an inspiration, others a coworkers or work friend. If you were to ask another group of people, they may say a prayer warrior, a pew mate, a college friend, a line sister, a sorority sister, a classmate, or a social media friend that they have never met in real life. If you know her well then you know she takes pride in being a mother, daughter, sister, aunt, niece, and cousin. Raine was named after her maternal grandmother, Florine and she has her aunt's middle name. Since both of these ladies have fallen eternally asleep, Raine has the pleasure of honoring them with her life while making sure her mother sees a return on her hard work, faith and tears.

Who is Raine as a person? God fearing, loving, strong-willed, determined, thoughtful, compassionate, forgiving, and fun. Raine was raised by her mother on the Southside of Fort Worth, her mother instilled in her drive and the love of God. Without this foundation, Raine wouldn't have survived half of what she faced in her adult life. Watching her mother go to school, work two jobs, and be active in church was one of the greatest life lessons that Raine could ever learn. It was through this that Raine became a lifelong learner. It was going to church all the time for Sunday School, Morning

Service, Evening Service, Wednesday Night Bible Study, Homecomings, Bible Bowls, and many other events that gave Raine her commitment to God. In her younger years, she just felt like it was just something that her mom made her do but as she began going through storms, she learned these events taught her more about her Heavenly Father! Praise God for mothers, especially mothers who teach the greatest lessons with life. This is why motherhood is such an important ministry to Raine.

Who is Raine the corporate employee? The author and writer? By profession, Raine is an analyst with one of the top auto insurers in the country for 15 years. An analyst by day and creative writer all the time, Raine, has a mission to be a voice of encouragement each day. Love of writing, came from her late aunt Michelle Williams. One of her life missions is to remind people that pain is temporary but their purpose is forever.

Raine has written many poems, motivational quotes, and Bible plans. She continues to branch out in the areas of books, more to come. She is an active presenter who has spoken at several lady's empowerment events. These moments only fuel her purpose to continue writing and speaking.

Who is Raine the lifelong learner? Raine holds a Bachelor's degree in Business Administration and Master's Degree in Education, she also holds several insurance designations including Chartered Life

Underwriter and her Life/Health license. She has a goal to empower others through her writing and education. She prides herself on being a lifelong learner. Although Raine has many credentials the most important thing she wants to be known for is being a Christian. Without Christ she is nothing.

Who is Raine as a mother? Motherhood is ministry, it is one that not everyone will be blessed to experience. So, for those who have the opportunity to become one it should not be taken lightly. Raine has two children, Mia and Michael, she is very active in their lives. Raine had a very good example and takes that same pride in making sure her kids have a great foundation and childhood. As a mother, Raine has been the team mom for peewee football, the mother who waits to make sure all the kids are picked up or who picks up the kids who need a ride. Raine is the volunteer at many afterschool games and programs, no task is too small from cleanup crew to manning the concession stand. The interactions at schools with the teachers, coaches, and other parents contributes to a greater community. It takes a village to raise children but first parents must be engaged.

Raine is the mother who sits in the cold during football season or in the heat during track season. Raine is the mother who will make sure all the teachers have a gift during teachers' appreciation week and Christmas. Raine is the mother who walks the halls at night to pray over her children. She is the mother who will stay up all night to cuddle sick children. Raine is the mother who will drive miles across town to take her children to enrichment programs and church events. If it brings a smile to her children's face it is worth every mile. While this may be time consuming it is an investment into a bright future.

Raine's children affectionately known as the M&Ms are her motivation. Everyone needs something to keep them going. Motherhood has taught Raine to never stop accomplishing goals, never quit when hard times come, and to never settle for less. Children have a way of bringing out a love and sense of drive that only children can do. During her time as a mother, she has earned a master's degree, insurance designations and licenses, and a life coaching certification.

Along with her successes her children have witnessed her overcome many challenges. It is because of them that she overcame them. Those challenges included back-to-back deaths, financial losses, divorce, relationship feud, and her fight with anxiety. They were her motivation. It was imperative that Raine showed her children how to be resilient, how to mourn, how to never quit, how to love, how to forgive but most importantly, how to trust God in the midst of a hot mess.

Who is Raine the family person? Daughter, Sister, Aunt, Niece, and Cousin. All these important roles. Family is usually defined by DNA but not with Raine.

Family is defined by the love and the blood of Christ. Raine has a loyalty to family which can sometimes be her weakness. One of the things that fills her cup is being there for her family. This doesn't mean attending every event or being everyone's beckon call, it means two things to Raine being there when she is needed the most and leaving her print of love for her loved ones.

One of the strengths Raine walks in is compassion with a tender heart. So, what does that look like for Raine? There have been long nights of friends who have laid on her couch because they were heavy hearted and knew Raine would fill their cup. Raine is one to randomly send messages of affirmation to her loved ones.

Family is an area that has brought many life lessons for Raine. One thing no one has control is the family they are born into. Your family will either be a blessing or a lesson but you get to choose how you react to it. For Raine it has been a bit of both but one lesson she has learned and wants to pass down to her children, nieces, and nephews is that love covers a multitude. It means that love never brags, love doesn't knowingly hurt, and love endures.

Raine loves hard especially once she had deemed you as family. She is the fun auntie, the one who wants to be a safe place for all of her nieces and nephews. It is vital to her that she is their safe place. She is the sister who loves her sisters, especially after the loss of her older brother. It is a reminder that death respects no one and doesn't care about plans. She is a cousin who will run around with the smaller cousins, she will color and play games with them all night. Whatever it takes to make them laugh. Laughter is good for the soul. She is the godmother who considered it an honor to be in this role. To be trusted with someone so precious is a blessing.

Being the best daughter to her mother is a lifelong mission. To watch someone, give all they had and wanting nothing in return but for her daughter to be the best, it is a no brainer to make sure that someone sees a return on their investment.

Who is Raine the Survivor? Everyone has survived something doesn't matter if it is outwardly discussed but it is the challenges that make everyone human. Pain may be caused from different sources but it feels the same. Raine has survived many things but those things give her the opportunity to connect with more people. To help more people, encourage more people, and remind them God is real and pain won't always last.

Raine is no stranger to hard times and challenges, in fact it is in these moments this is where Raine realized she needed to be the voice of reason for someone else. She wants to be what she needed in some of the darkest moments of her life.

What does a survivor do? Survive! From 2012 to

2014, life began to spin for so many different reasons, her marriage was off, she had been passed over for promotion after promotion. This led to her having panic attacks, asthma attacks, and migraines.

In 2014, she went through a divorce, one of the most hurtful pain ever, no one gets married to end it in divorce. But Raine survived.

In 2015, Raine began to self-medicate with shopping and partying which led to making bad decisions, ones that she is not proud of. In November, she lost a dear friend to Cancer, two weeks after that she lost a grandmother, and two weeks after that she lost a friend to a natural disaster. But Raine survived.

In 2016, she had two surgeries in the same year. She found a lump in the right breast and although it was noncancerous, it had to be removed for fear of that changing, unexpected surgeries and bills. In November, she watched her sweet great grandmother fight and fight, one day in the hospital she told her she was ready to go, can you imagine having to carry that and not telling anyone else? In December, the spiral of back-to-back deaths began again, but the one that hurt the most was her older brother who was only 35. But Raine survived.

In 2017, Raine relocated my family from their comfort zone and it has turned out to be one of the greatest blessings. And she survived.

In 2018, Raine had many accomplishments but all she can remember is that death struck again, her aunt, her second mom. But Raine survived.

Raine decided that the darkest moments are only for a season. You can either remain in faith and watch rain turn to rainbows or come into agreement with failure, depression, suicide, self-pity, bitterness, unforgiveness, self-hate, and envy. Raine turned all of these challenges into purpose. One of her quotes was birthed during this process: "My identity is not defined by my trials but in my trials, I found my identity."

Who is Raine the encourager? The Life Coach? The inspiration? It is sometimes in AFFLICTION, that you find CONVICTION, which leads to a clearer DEPICTION that your current circumstances can't last always and your faith is a hopeful PREDICTION that prompts you to cast t out the enemy and his RESTRICTIONS because God gave you PERMISSION to be great and anything less that than is FICTION.

Raine, the survivor turned into Raine the encourager, the life coach, and what some people may deem as an inspiration. This includes overcoming dark moments. Dark moments include surviving infidelity in marriage that led to divorce. Dark moments included the lack of financial wisdom and making bad decisions. Dark moments include watching loved one's transition, literally watching loved ones fight for their life. Dark moments include fighting anxiety and panic attacks. Dark moments include self-esteem issues. Dark moments include reliving childhood hurts.

Dark moments don't last, in fact they gave birth to Raine's purpose. She is now devoted to being a light in dark moments and in a world that needs lighter. Why throw shade when you can be the light?

Each day, you can follow Raine on Instagram and Facebook as RaineRealities. On these pages you will find quotes and inspiration to keep going. Those words may be the very words that a stranger needs to see to know that God didn't bring them this far to only bring them this far. Through these inspiration pages she is able to reach people all over the world. While some may want a platform to be seen, Raine just wants the one person who feels alone, who wants to quit, who feels God doesn't hear them to run across one of her posts and remember whom they are in God. If the page only saves one soul, mission accomplished.

In 2020, Raine became a certified life coach, through this platform she is able to assist single moms, career seeking women, and women coping with divorce. As a life coach, she is devoted to holding others accountable to becoming their best self.

As a certified life coach, she is committed to being a trusted coach for the journey. It will indeed be a journey, be sure to give yourself some grace throughout this process. She is honored to celebrate your efforts along the way and be as excited and committed as they are being accomplished. If you are interested in discussing life coaching options send an email to rainerealities@gmail.com.

What Does Raine Value? What Can You Expect from Her? Raine is dedicated to adding value in all that she does, in any department she works in, in any book she writes in, and any things else God blesses her to do. What she enjoys most is building relationships, helping business partners, clients, and mentees accomplish their goals, and leading others. It is hard not to smile or laugh when she is present, she brings a positive vibe and can-do spirit.

Raine enjoys collaboration where everyone's voice is heard to achieve results. Teamwork where everyone understands their role and takes ownership of their actions while celebrating wins and figuring out how to overcome challenges. Optimistic attitudes, Raine will always see the positive in all situations. What you can expect from Raine is transparency, a leader, a lifelong learner, laughter, honesty, and commitment. Raine is a trustworthy motivator, a dependable resource, often works with little no direction from leadership, and devoted to the forward movement of anything she is blessed to be a part of.

How to contact Raine? RaineRealities@gmail.com , follow her on Instagram at RaineRealities, and like her on Facebook at Raine Realties.

Michelle Herbert

Optimist, Missionary & Mother

Michelle Herbert's life is all about family, church, friends...and spreading the good news.

Michelle lives at the water's edge in the beautiful Pacific Northwest. She thrives on worshipping and praising God. She loves to travel, hike and explore God's amazing world. She has appeared on television, radio, modeled and traveled God's beautiful world on the stage. She has said no to Hollywood twice in order to put God first. She enjoys storytelling, speaking, teaching and writing. Michelle is an alumni of York College, Oklahoma Christian University via their Cascade College campus, and Sunset International Bible Institute. From the very start, she loved to tell stories and carry people through dramatic tales of adventure, hope and love. Her life celebrates the power of God's grace and boundless love through tragedy, life and even in death. Today, she is a Women's Ministry Leader in Seattle, Wa and a Spiritual Life Discipline's Coach. Michelle enjoys the power of prayer, the proclamation of worship and praise, the heralding of the Word of God, memorizing and reciting scripture and holds dear to the glorious experience of fasting. Michelle has worshipped through many extended and short-term fasts. Fasting, teaches us so many wonderful truths about ourselves and our Lord and Savior. Fasting can radically change your life and walk with God. Through fasting, prayer and worship we can overcome the spiritual obstacles in our lives. Michelle writes, we can restore, strengthen and regain our hopes, dreams and walk with God through prayer, fasting, worshipping and praising God. The author is a missionary, teacher, speaker, an avid hiker, amateur photographer, blessed mother of seven, a first-time grandma, trusted friend, charmed wife, crochet queen, sharpshooter, good listener and terrible at the art of sitting still. She lives a ferry boat away from adventure on the waters of Puget Sound, where she divides her time between faith, family and friends.

Personal Message from Michelle:

I am a Michelle and I am a miracle. I was created out of the love of God. I am a Missionary, a Church Planter, and a Women's Ministry Leader. I have one quest in my life. I desire to worship God. I mean really worship God. One day, I will join him in heaven. I will bow before his throne. One day, my body will be transformed and I will praise him, eternally. My voice will never grow faint or hoarse. I will stand beside my brothers and sisters in Christ and proclaim Jesus Christ is the King of Kings. I know the power of his love and his greatness because I have been saved from sin and death. What exactly is greatness? God is the ultimate representation of greatness! Jesus was born into this sinful world. In his selflessness, he overcame sin and death. He lives and he is preparing a place for me. A place not of this world. A place in heaven. I wanted to be a part of him. He now lives with me.

From a young age, I knew I wanted to be a follower of Christ. A woman of God. A loving mother. A faithful wife. I gathered my convictions from the good examples and experiences in my life. I remember praying at a young age to God. At my request, my mother would drop me off at church. At five years old, I was sitting in church by myself. I hoped I would not miss a word the preacher was teaching us.

Honestly, I was born into chaos. If you know me and you are reading this. Be prepared. This is my testimony. It is not where I dwell. I want to share the events and the people who have influenced my life. Some are good and some are bad. All of the people I mention, I love very dearly. I appreciate the moments of kindness and love we shared at some point in my life.

As a child, my father introduced me to his lover and to the unborn child in her belly. I remember the last day my father hit my mother. My father was living out his family curse. He was a victim of abuse and alcohol consumed his young adult life. I knew from that moment. I would never tolerate a man hitting or cheating on me. Praise God, my father has recovered from alcoholism and he has been redeemed. He has dedicated his life to helping others, who struggle with addiction.

My mother is a loving mother. She is the homecoming princess, kind, sweet and smart. She is a mama bear. She is a survivor of abuse. I can remember the day my step-father locked my mother in their room. It seemed like days. He yelled at her over and over again.

He often yelled. He had his own addictions and pain. When I went in to see her. She was crying. I was very familiar with my mother's tears. Although, I can't recall what the argument was about. It never mattered to me. I just wanted the yelling to stop. I walked into her room and found her reading her bible. Those are the moments that focused me. Those are the moments ingrained and seared in my mind. Those are the moments that changed me. Throughout my life, whenever I saw tears, I saw the Bible being opened.

When I was a child, two of my uncles would hide food in my coat. At various times in my life, I remember them using my innocence to conceal their stealing. I didn't know it at the time. They were quiet and crafty in the moment. Their thrills revealed their deceit after the fact. I can remember taking candy at a young age. My youngest uncle spanked me, as my grandfather watched. He loved the Bible. I often saw my uncle reading the Bible. He suffered a major head injury. He jumped. He was hit in the head with a bat. He came to live with us after his accident. He struggled to hold onto his mental health after his head injury. He lost his life at a young age. I was determined to love my life and the Bible.

My grandfather was my hero. My grandmother was a. a wonderful example of motherhood and an amazing wife. They took me to church. They told me about God. Grandfather read his bible in front of me and he read the Bible to me. My grandfather and grandmother were faithful. He died when I was child.

Yet, his influence has always grounded me. My grandmother continued to reinforce my grandfather's love for preaching and teaching the Word God. I would catch them reading the Bible in their humble home. I knew one day I would read the Bible to my children.

I would beg my mother to take me to church. My mother made sure I was at church, even if she did not go. She was embarrassed because my stepfather would rarely go to church. She would often cry, as she sat alone in church. My mother went to church because she found the family of God at church. Mom would open her bible with the elders and their wives, the Preacher and his wife and ladies of the church. Mom would find God's peace at our family church.

What is my greatness? My strength. My strength comes out of my weakness. My mother was one of my heroes as a child. Deep down, I wanted to grow up and be a mother, just like my mom. She was beautiful and always there for me. She was a stay-at-home mother for a time. I loved that. But, she always seemed to be missing something and it broke my heart.

What was the day that it all caved in on me? I can remember going to church with my mother after my stepfather held her up in her bedroom. I loved to touch her long hair. She always sat alone at church unless she sat with someone else. She wanted her husband to sit beside her and it broke her heart. I realized I wanted a husband who sat. beside me church every Sunday.my husband was saved. He came to church, most of the time. But, it was then, I wondered, would my children really see my husband and I worshipping God and worshipping Him?

My weakness was my family. Yes, my greatest desire was to be a part of the family of God. I wanted to raise my children in the Lord. I saw many of my uncles and cousins hooked on drugs, alcohol and in prison, throughout my life. I knew through the Word of God and through the church, I could have a family who would worship God with me. I could have a family who not only sit beside me in church but who would sit beside me in heaven. I want to sit with Jesus and with my family in heaven.

My young husband was a friend to all. He had friends who stopped by all the time. If they stopped by on Sunday morning. He would visit with them and I would go to church. I had to challenge that for my dream to be realized. I had to challenge that for my survival. I prayed. I got the kids ready and we loaded everything up in the car for church, no matter who came by. It was tough, saying goodbye to friends in our driveway. But, God was there for us. Our habits changed. Brother Ken greeted my husband over and over again. Brother Ken was that man who shook your hand a bit longer and talked with you because he really cared. He knew Jesus wanted my husband to be a part of the church, not just to go to church.

My husband was a natural servant and leader. He was soon asked to serve as a deacon. He loved being a part of the family of God. He was committed. My husband loved to open his bible. He loved to teach the Word of God. He committed to sitting with me in church, for the rest of his life. My husband committed to inviting other people into the family of God. He committed to opening his bible daily. He still sits by me in church, but he gets up to serve the church and to preach the Word.

So here I am. I am determined to raise my children with the love for God. My eldest son recently asked me how my husband and I got together. We are an unlikely couple and we don't have a romantic love story. The odds were definitely against us. We met on the stage. My husband's father died when he was a boy, before he knew Jesus. Apparently, He was a bit of a troubled teen. I only saw a young man that was student of the month, the lead actor in all the plays, constantly on the cover of our local newspaper, a champion marksman, a recipient of a full scholarship and a friend to all. I'm not trying to sell him. He was pretty amazing. He likes to think how amazing it is that we found each other. We were an unlikely couple. After, I had my heart to heart with my son. He said, "Wow, mom! Thank you for telling me. That is not at all how you raised us." It was a compliment. My son saw that we conquered our family curse. My son was going to be different because he had lived a different story.

I am a spiritual life coach. I have followed my life's obsession. My life's goal is to be a follower of Christ. I am an optimist. No one knows me as a victim or survivor. I don't talk poorly of my parents. I love them, for what they have overcome. I live in joy. I am known for my joy. My joy bothers people at times. Some would prefer I live in a world where things are not ok. Where I hash out my sorrows. I cannot. I know who I am. I know where I have come from. I know where I have fallen. I know how to get up. For me, every morning is wonderful. It's an opportunity to do good, to accomplish the tasks ahead, to serve God, to do great things and to love.

My eight year old son tells me scripture to brighten my day. "Mom, God doesn't give us more than we can handle." 1 Corinthians 10:13. My eldest son wanted to be a preacher when he was just five years old. He became a missionary at eighteen and he is preaching the gospel. My oldest daughter fell in love with a missionary while, studying to be a missionary for the deaf. She became a mother this year. A wonderful mother. It is not uncommon for parents to discourage their children to be in ministry. It is not a glamours, wealthy nor highly honored position to be in ministry, according to the world. But, I welcome it wholeheartedly. My kids found their own drive, their own faith and their own determination.

My desire is for all my children is to seek the face of God and worship him. My family, friends and church are who I treasure. They complete me. I was born into a world filled with chaos. I will live as if I have been redeemed. I desire to worship God daily.

I enjoy memorizing and studying the Word of God. When I am happy and productive, I want to be caught with my Bible open. When my tears fall, I want to be caught with my bible open. I was born in Seattle. I was raised on a ferry boat away from the city. I have many family members who found drugs on the streets of Seattle. I have lost other family members to the streets of Seattle. Today, I am ministering to those same streets. I minister in the same neighborhoods where my family members were lost to drugs. I am ministering to the homeless on the streets where I lost some of my own family members. I have been able to help get someone off of the streets. I've been able to baptize someone in the same waters that a body was found, earlier this summer. I am giving back to this city. My faith legacy started with my grandfather and my grandmother. I hope to find people who will one day share their faith with their children and grandchildren.

The Northwest is home to many bald eagles. One of my favorite verses is, "Yet those who wait for the Lord will gain new strength; They will mount up with wings like eagles, They will run and not get tired, They will walk and not become weary," Isaiah 40:31. My hope is not of this world. My hope lies in the name of the Lord. Everyday, I wish to mount up and take flight with renewed strength from the Lord. I want to look forward with great vision. My life is renewed, daily. My spirit sours because Jesus is with me. He never leaves my side. I am holding onto the hope of my youth. I am seeking his face daily. I long to worship the king of Kings before his throne. I am His servant. I am a mother and a wife. We read the bible and worship God.

I am Michelle Herbert...

Dr Nadia Watson-Anthony, Ph.D

Philanthropist, Entrepreneur & Ambassador

Dr Nadia Watson-Anthony helps women world-wide take their vision and makes it their reality through sound strategy development. She intuitively sees the threads of opportunity that wind through an organization, ministry and business. Nadia works to bring these three together into a coherent whole, helping others extend their thinking, and drives positive advantages.

Dr Anthony is an inspirational leader who tells stories that inspire action while at the same time is grounded in information that gives leverage to anyone that crosses her path. Respected as a credible voice in decision making. She leads mainly by example, always doing her best and encouraging others to do the same.

Currently, as Executive Director at "Sunrise Women's Clinic, Nadia commits to the vision providing top-level insight, inspiration, information. Dr Nadia also contributes to raising financial support to provide staff income and free medical services for pregnant women and children.

In addition to these excellent opportunities, (Nadia Anthony) stands behind thousands of podiums speaking to audiences of people concerning Biblical Truth and in support of her local pregnancy center "Sunrise Women's Clinic."

In the Hills of Sidney, her goal is to lead a session at workshops, conventions and meetings, gathering of thousands of leaders teaching them how they can support the local mission (pregnancy center) and it's staff along with anti-abortion leaders from across the country.

After graduation in 2017 Nadia worked cleaning the local Church of Christ while pregnant with her fifth child. This experience forced her to seek god's purpose for her life.

Simultaneous, Nadia discovered her passion for the church (women and girls) and inspiring others to see the bigger picture of life. After searching for opportunity in the communities of Wills Point Texas, an opportunity presented itself for Nadia to work with the local City officials. Months went by and it seems as though the lord took his hands-off Nadia.

Until one day during a hot summer day the lord spoke to Nadia concerning her writing a 31 day devotion. The lord gave Nadia a nudge to write this book. After publication the lord nudged Nadia again to take a second look at the title. With great joy finally, Nadia began to leap for joy because the book God named " HER INSPIRATION" was going to make room for Nadia's ego. Well, it did not quite work out that way, Nadia received a third nudge that informed her the titled book " HER INSPIRATION" was not about her, but about all the women she would encounter and help.

With this Godly insight from the throne room of God, Nadia founded "HER INSPIRATION" in

2019 which is a platform for spiritually practical encouragement for women and girls. Dr Anthony's vision is to lead individuals in developing a more authentic and fervent spiritual life through speaking and book writing, providing safe havens and needs to communities across the world. Nadia's mission is to teach and exemplify this: "give yourself GRACE, Love Serve and Sacrifice with Passion."

Dr Nadia Graduated from Sunset Bible Institution holding a ABS, Nadia continued her education by attending Amridge University graduating with a B.S.M, M.S.W, and Ph.D from UGCSI. Dr Nadia Anthony was placed as the Fundraising Lead for SAVEmondak MT&ND organization that focus on suicide awareness. In 2019 Nadia collaborated eight-teen women who became co-authors of her Anthology ``Women to Women." Year of the pandemic, 2020 she collaborated with 16 Women for "THE HiddenFigures Book. Dr Anthony is the founder of Christian Maturity Mentorship Program, Sponsor for the American Foundation for Suicide Prevention, Donates to a Mission (yearly ladies' day) in Togo West Africa F.A.W.M.- (French **Africa Women Ministry)** Great contributor of Sunrise Women's Clinic, Book writing Ambassador for Greatness University of London, UK.

Member of the Global Library of Female Authors (TGLFA) this is a library of females that have created and established programs to enhance the lives of other females globally.

Dr Anthony was Nominated for a Humanitarian civility award. Inducted in the first of its kind, "Worlds book of Greatness 2020." Inducted in "The worlds book of Greatness 2021" she is the first ever Greatness Ambassador in Montana USA.

Dr Anthony has written several books, "H.E.R. Inspiration 31 day devotion," "Women to Women "transitioning into your best future," "Women to Women Sisters of Sarah," "The Book of Love" and has co-author varies of books (BEST SELLERS)," Jesus changed our lives" and "Les Brown changed our lives."

In between traveling Nadia volunteers for speaking engagements at nursing facilities and schools. Nadia is passionate about all creation, education, leadership, empowerment, and her faith. Dr Anthony understands that power has been continuously abused for personal gains and profit.

That is why she works hard giving women equal opportunities to become Authors and be the best of themselves they could possibly be. Nadia is convinced women supporting women is on the rise and has been on the rise for years.

Nadia Believes that this empowerment will give access to natural and intellectual resources, possibility and opportunities to produce, build and dominate. Nadia believes that everyone should at least write one book in their lifetime. Nadia has done mission work in New Mexico, Montana and in the largest Muslim community in the United States (Dearborn, Michigan).

Nadia is happily married to her husband Dr. Charles Anthony with a blended family of nine.

Quote
"In order to be a great Individual, one must read and educate themselves on all areas of life."— Nadia Anthony.

Future projects:

- Body Transformation Book with Kim "FITKUPKAKE" Kauffman THE TRAINER
- "Girl, give yourself Grace" with Michelle Frank MSN, APRN, CNP
- "What is Philanthropy"

23 things about DR. Nadia "SUGA" Anthony LOVES

1. Working for the lord
2. Supporting husband so much!
3. Reading to her children
4. Doing comedy with her children
5. Dancing
6. Music; Blues, R&B, JaZZ AND COUNTRY
7. Hallmark channel

8. Reading near a fireplace
9. Trying on clothes in her home boutique
10. Taking pictures, editing pictures
11. Writing books
12. Encouraging women and girls
13. Challenging men to see women in different perspectives
14. Making her home look like a magazine cover
15. Driving her 2 seater car in the summertime
16. Trying to sing with her husband.
17. Red wine occasionally with pasta
18. Being around uplifting women
19. Working out
20. Eating healthy
21. Elderly people
22. Giving meaningful gifts
23. And lastly loves being versatile with her dressing and hair...

www.nadiaanthony.org

H.E.R INSPIRATION STANDS FOR HEALING, EDIFICATION AND REST.

Pandemic History

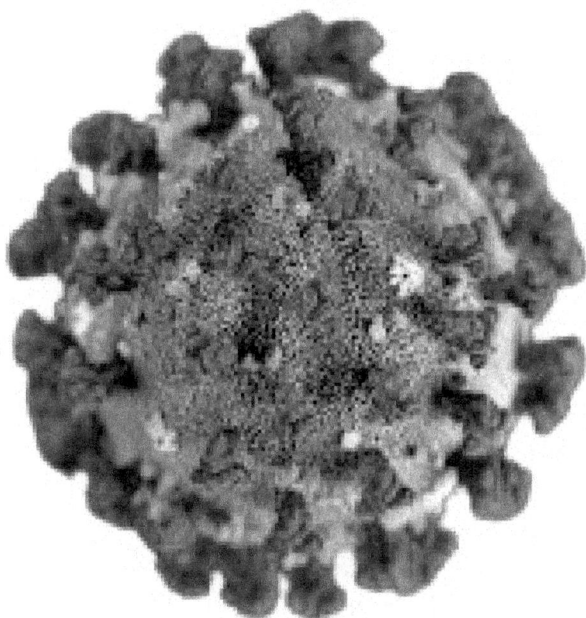

Hidden Figures

January 9 — WHO Announces Mysterious Coronavirus-Related Pneumonia in Wuhan, China

January 21 — CDC Confirms First US Coronavirus Case

January 23 — Wuhan Now Under Quarantine

January 31 — WHO Issues Global Health Emergency

February 2 — Global Air Travel Is Restricted

February 3 — US Declares Public Health Emergency

February 10 — China's COVID-19 Deaths Exceed Those of SARS Crisis

February 25 — CDC Says COVID-19 Is Heading Toward Pandemic Status

March 6 — 21 Passengers on California Cruise Ship Test Positive

March 11 — WHO Declares COVID-19 a Pandemic

March 13 — Trump Declares COVID-19 a National Emergency

March 13 — Travel Ban on Non-US Citizens Traveling From Europe Goes Into Effect

March 17 — University of Minnesota Begins Testing Hydroxychloroquine

March 17 — CMS Temporarily Expands Use of Telehealth

March 17 — Administration Asks Congress to Send Americans Direct Financial Relief

March 19 — California Issues Statewide Stay-at-Home Order

March 24 — With Clinical Trials on Hold, Innovation Stalls

Packed hospitals trying to keep out everyone who does not need to be there, and that means delays.

March 25 — Reports Find Extended Shutdowns Can Delay Second Wave

March 26 — Senate Passes CARES Act

March 27 — President Trump Signs CARES Act Into Law

The House of Representatives approves the CARES act, the largest economic recovery package in history, and President Trump signs it into law. The bipartisan legislation provides direct payments to Americans and expansions in unemployment insurance.

March 30 — FDA Authorizes Use of
Hydroxychloroquine

March 31 — COVID-19 Can Be Transmitted
Through the Eye

A report in JAMA Ophthalmology creates a stir with
the finding that patients can catch the virus that
causes COVID-19 through the eye, despite low
prevalence of the virus in tears.

April 8 — Troubles With the COVID-19 Cocktail

"What do you have to lose?" Trump asks when
touting the malaria drug hydroxycholorquine or the
related chloroquine as possible treatments for
COVID-19.

April 16 — "Gating Criteria" Emerge as a Way to
Reopen the Economy

April 28 — Young, Poor Avoid Care for COVID-19
Symptoms

April 29 — NIH Trial Shows Early Promise for
Remdesivir

May 1 — Remdesivir Wins EUA

May 9 — Saliva-Based Diagnostic Test Allowed for
At-Home Use

May 12 — Death Toll Likely Underestimated, Fauci

Testifies

May 21 — United States and AstraZeneca Form Vaccine Deal

May 28 — US COVID-19 Deaths Pass the 100,000 Mark

June 4 — Lancet, NEJM Retract COVID-19 Studies on Hydroxychloroquine

June 10 — US COVID-19 Cases Reach 2 Million

June 16 — HHS Announces COVID-19 Vaccine Doses Will Be Free for Some

June 18 — WHO Ends Study Into Hydroxychloroquine

June 20 — NIH Halts Trial of Hydroxychloroquine

June 22 — Study Suggests 80% of Cases in March Went Undetected

June 26 — White House Coronavirus Task Force Addresses Rising Cases in the South

June 29 — Gilead Sets Price for Remdesivir at $3120

June 30 — Fauci Warns New COVID-19 Cases Could Hit 100,000 a Day

July 2 — States Reverse Reopening Plans

July 6 — Scientists, Citing Airborne Transmission, Ask WHO to Revise Guidance

July 7 — CMS Plans to Pay More for Home Dialysis Equipment

July 7 — US Surpasses 3 Million Infections, Begins WHO Withdrawal

July 9 — WHO Announces COVID-19 Can Be Airborne

July 14 — States With COVID-19 Spikes Report Greatest Health Insurance Coverage Losses

July 14 — Early Moderna Data Point to Vaccine Candidate's Efficacy

July 15 — New Hospital Data Reporting Protocol Prompts Concern

July 16 — US Reports New Record of Daily COVID-19 Cases

July 20 — Diagnostic Delays From COVID-19 May Increase Cancer-Related Deaths

The next several years could bear witness to thousands of additional deaths from cancer that could have been.

July 21 — Vaccines From AstraZeneca, CanSino Biologics Show Promising Results

July 22 — HHS, DOD Announce Vaccine
Distribution Agreement With Pfizer and BioNTech

July 23 — Antibody Levels Drop After First 3
Months of COVID-19 Infection

July 23 — Antibody Cocktail May Treat, Prevent
COVID-19

July 27 — Moderna Vaccine Begins Phase 3 Trial,
Receives $472M From Trump Administration

July 27 — Senate Introduces HEALS Act

July 29 — FDA Grants Truvian EUA for Rapid
Antibody Test

August 3 — New US Pandemic Phase; US to Pay
Sanofi, GlaxoSmithKline $2B for Vaccine

August 4 — Rural Hotspots Face Lack of Intensive
Care Unit Beds

August 7 — Talks Stall on Second Relief Package

August 11 — Trump Administration Reaches Deal
With Moderna

August 12 — Severe Obesity Increases Mortality
Risk From COVID-19

August 13 — Biden Calls for 3-Month Mask
Mandate

August 15 — FDA Approves Saliva Test

August 17 — COVID-19 Now the Third-Leading Cause of Death in the US

August 23 — Convalescent Plasma Is Cleared for Use by FDA

August 24 — Remdesivir's Clinical Benefits Questioned

August 25 — CDC Changes Testing Guidance, but Later Reverses Itself

August 26 — FDA Grants EUA to Abbott's Rapid Test

August 28 — First Known Case of COVID-19 Reinfection Reported in the US

September 1 — US Rejects WHO Global COVID-19 Vaccine Effort

September 3 — Steroids Reduce Mortality in Severe Cases; Sanofi, GSK Begin Human Vaccine Trials

September 3 — Bioethicists Weigh In on Equitable Vaccine Distribution

September 8 — AstraZeneca Halts Phase 3 Vaccine Trial

September 14 — US Airports Stop Screening

Hidden Figures

International Travelers

September 14 — Pfizer, BioNTech Expand Phase 3 Trial

September 14 — NIH Launches Investigation Into Halted Astrazeneca Trial

September 15 — CDC Reports on Spread of COVID-19 at Restaurants

September 16 — Trump Administration Releases Vaccine Distribution Plan

September 17 — Europe Reports Rising COVID-19 Cases

September 21 — CDC Pulls Guidance Saying COVID-19 Transmission Is Airborne

September 21 — Johnson & Johnson Begins Phase 3 Vaccine Trial

September 23 — A New, More Contagious Strain of COVID-19 Is Discovered

September 25 — Midwest States See Increase in COVID-19 Cases

September 28 — Global COVID-19 Deaths Surpass 1 Million

September 29 — HHS to Distribute 100 Million

Rapid Tests to States

September 29 — Regeneron Announces Positive Results for Monoclonal Antibody Treatment

October 2 — Trump, First Lady Test Positive for COVID-19; Trump Enters Hospital

October 5 — Trump Leaves Hospital, Continues Receiving Treatment

October 8 — NEJM Criticizes Trump's COVID-19 Response; 39 States See Case Spikes

October 8 — More Americans Trust Biden to Lead Health Care System

October 8 — White House COVID-19 Outbreak Grows to 34

October 9 — US Signs Deal With AstraZeneca

October 12 — Johnson & Johnson Halts Vaccine Trial

October 15 — US Cases Spike Again; Studies Connect Blood Type and COVID-19 Risk

October 19 — Global Cases Top 40 Million

October 22 — FDA Approves Remdesivir as First COVID-19 Drug

October 23 — AstraZeneca and Johnson & Johnson Announce Restart of COVID-19 Vaccine Trials

October 11, and a patient in the AstraZeneca trial developed neurological symptoms before its study was halted on September 6. An independent monitoring committee determined that the trial for the latter vaccine candidate was safe to continue.

October 28 — CMS Issues Vaccine, Treatment Coverage Rules

November 4 — US Reports Unprecedented 100,000 Cases in 1 Day

November 5 — Study Predicts Difficulties in Nationwide COVID-19 Immunity

November 9 — President-Elect Biden Announces COVID-19 Transition Team; Pfizer Publishes Vaccine Results

November 9 — FDA Issues EUA for Eli Lilly's Antibody Treatment

November 11 — Indoor Venues Responsible for Much of COVID-19's Spread

November 16 — Moderna Reveals Vaccine Efficacy Results

November 16 — FDA to Move Rapidly on EUAs

for Pfizer, Moderna Vaccines

November 17 — Fauci Highlights the Need for Long-term Follow-up of COVID-19 Effects

November 18 — Pfizer, BioNTech Vaccine Is 95% Effective

November 20 — Pfizer, BioNTech Submit EUA Application; CDC Warns Against Holiday Travel

November 23 — AstraZeneca Reports Vaccine Is 90% Effective; FDA Grants EUA for Second Antibody Treatment

This information has to been provided by [AJMC]

www.ingramcontent.com/pod-product-compliance
Lightning Source LLC
Chambersburg PA
CBHW060529210326
41519CB00014B/3172